I0189158

IMAGES
of Rail

THE CHICAGO GREAT WESTERN RAILWAY

The following places are labeled on the map:

MINNEAPOLIS, ST. PAUL, SOUTH ST. PAUL, RED WING, FARIBAULT, ROCHESTER, MANKATO, WINONA, WISCONSIN, AUSTIN, MASON CITY, NEW HAMPTON, OSAGE, CLARION, OELWEIN, DYERSVILLE, DUBUQUE, FORT DODGE, HAMPTON, WAVERLY, CEDAR FALLS, WATERLOO, SYCAMORE, CARROL, MARSHALLTOWN, DE KALB, MAYWOOD, CHICAGO, DES MOINES, COUNCIL BLUFFS, OMAHA, IOWA, ILLINOIS, SAVANNAH, ST. JOSEPH, MISSOURI, LEAVENWORTH, KANS., KANSAS CITY, KANSAS CITY

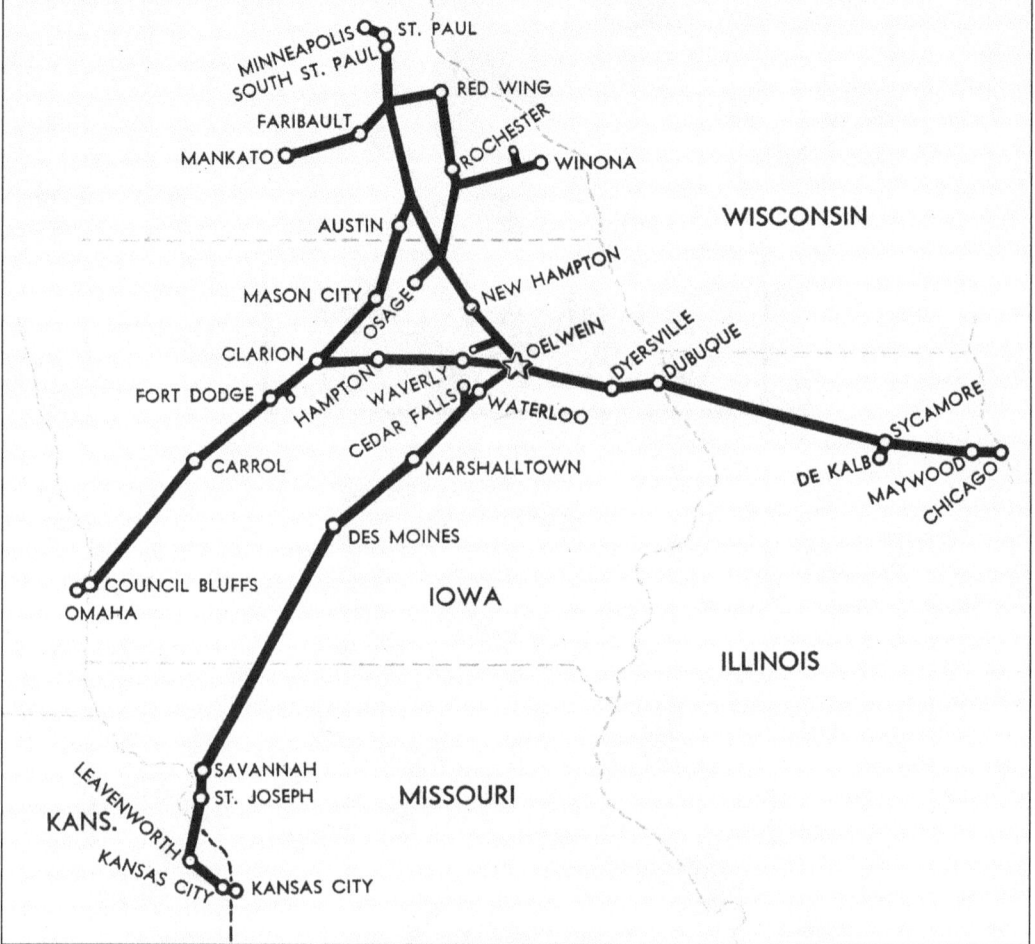

This stylized map of the Chicago Great Western (CGW) Railway system was published in the company's 1957 annual report. The main lines formed a misshapen letter *x* or plus sign, with one line between Minneapolis–St. Paul and Kansas City, and the other between Chicago and Omaha. The lines crossed at Oelwein, Iowa, the system hub, which included a classification yard and repair shops for rolling stock and locomotives. Although there were several branches, the system primarily consisted of main lines and connections with other railroads, which enabled the CGW to serve chiefly as a bridge carrier between railroads. The company operated 1,458 route miles of track divided into divisions and districts to facilitate managing operations. Illinois was located in the Eastern Division, which extended from Chicago to Oelwein. The division was renamed the Illinois Division in 1930 and renamed again as Eastern Division in the early 1950s. This complex organization moved 268,221 carloads of freight the same year the map was published.

On the cover: CGW steam locomotive No. 502 with passenger train was photographed crossing over the Des Plaines River Bridge west of Forest Park, Illinois, on March 16, 1919. (James L. Rueber.)

IMAGES
of Rail

THE CHICAGO GREAT
WESTERN RAILWAY

David J. Fiore Sr.

ARCADIA
PUBLISHING

Copyright © 2006 by David J. Fiore Sr.
ISBN 978-1-5316-2428-6

Published by Arcadia Publishing
Charleston, South Carolina

Library of Congress Catalog Card Number: 2006926360

For all general information contact Arcadia Publishing at:
Telephone 843-853-2070
Fax 843-853-0044
E-mail sales@arcadiapublishing.com
For customer service and orders:
Toll-Free 1-888-313-2665

Visit us on the Internet at www.arcadiapublishing.com

*This book is dedicated to my family
for their support and patience while I spent time away from
them researching and writing. And it is also dedicated to the former
employees of the Chicago Great Western Railway.*

CONTENTS

ACKNOWLEDGMENTS

I wish to acknowledge the following persons and institutions for their generous assistance: Sue Breese and the Joiner History Room, Sycamore, Illinois; James L. Rueber; Joseph Piersen and Fred Klinger with the Archives Sub-Committee of the Chicago and North Western Historical Society, Elmhurst, Illinois; Conrad "Pete" Pedersen; Donald Vaughn; Julie Bunke, St. Charles Heritage Center, St. Charles, Illinois; Dawn M. Johnson, Byron Museum of History; Carol Stream Historical Society, Carol Stream, Illinois; Elizabeth Historical Society, Elizabeth, Illinois; Villa Park Historical Society, Villa Park, Illinois; Lombard Historical Society, Lombard, Illinois; Jeff Ruetsche, editor, and John Pearson, publisher, Arcadia Publishing.

INTRODUCTION

On March 4, 1854, the Minnesota territorial legislature granted a charter to a group of Eastern capitalists to build the Minnesota and Northwestern Railroad (M&NW) between Lake Superior and Iowa. However, the M&NW was not completed due to a federal land grant scandal and the financial panic of 1857.

A. B. Stickney, a St. Paul railroad executive, acquired the charter in the early 1880s for the purpose of building a new rail line in the Midwest. Stickney's experience and managerial abilities combined with sufficient capital from local and foreign investors enabled the M&NW to start construction at St. Paul and Randolph, Minnesota, in September 1884. A year later, on September 20, 1885, the first train departed St. Paul for Chicago, which it reached through a convoluted route over three other railroads. By January 1, 1889, the M&NW was in operation with its own rails between Chicago, Minneapolis–St. Paul, and Kansas City. Further expansion occurred between July 1901 and November 1903, when the company increased its mileage in Minnesota and built an extension to Omaha.

Stickney achieved his goal through several methods, including incorporating companies that actually constructed railways, leasing property, and acquiring existing railroads. The Chicago, St. Paul and Kansas City Railway (CStP&KC), incorporated in Iowa on June 1, 1886, was one of the companies organized by Stickney. M&NW was subsequently deeded to CStP&KC on December 8, 1887, and, five years later, Stickney incorporated the first Chicago Great Western Railway (CGW) on January 16, 1892, to effect a financial reorganization of CStP&KC.

This first CGW relied upon debenture stock rather than bonds for capitalization, and Stickney proudly boasted in 1899 that the company was "a western trunk line railway without a mortgage." However, the CGW borrowed a substantial amount of money through promissory notes to finance improvements. In 1908, $8 million in notes came due, but CGW lacked the funds to pay its debt due to a decline in earnings in 1907. On January 8, 1908, CGW was placed into receivership.

On August 19, 1909, a syndicate organized by J. P. Morgan and Company incorporated a new company, Chicago Great Western *Railroad*, which purchased CGW *Railway* on August 21, 1909, for $12 million. Samuel M. Felton became president, and he began an extensive program of rehabilitation and improvements that totaled over $32 million by 1925.

Patrick H. Joyce, vice president of the Standard Steel Car Company, and a group of associates took an interest in the CGW during the late 1920s. They were aware that CGW had failed to pay dividends on its preferred stock at various times since 1909, and accumulations totaled $50 per share. They also knew that the company could pay the accumulation and resume regular dividends if earnings improved.

To provide the railroad with more business, transportation managers at various companies were solicited to purchase shares of stock in CGW and then route as much freight as possible over the line. The syndicate organized a holding company, Bremo Corporation, on January 5, 1929, and they eventually secured complete control of CGW through stock ownership by April 1930. Unfortunately, the new management conducted unethical business practices during the next two decades, which resulted in investigations by the Interstate Commerce Commission (ICC) and the federal Senate Committee on Interstate Commerce.

The combination of mismanagement and a business downturn due to the Great Depression forced CGW to file for bankruptcy on February 28, 1935. The reorganization process required six years to complete and included incorporation of the Chicago Great Western *Railway*, on April 22, 1940. CGW *Railway* took possession of CGW *Railroad* on February 19, 1941.

CGW experienced a significant decline in intercity freight and passenger business by the 1950s. The situation mirrored the predicament faced by the entire railroad industry at that time. Total mileage in service in the United States had reached an all-time high of 254,000 miles in 1916. At the same time, the trunk lines were transporting 77 percent of intercity freight traffic and 98 percent of intercity passenger traffic. These ratios declined to 46 percent and 31 percent, respectively, by 1957, as the industry lost business to other modes of transportation. There were simply too many railroads competing for limited business and, despite various efficiencies, the number of employees, locomotives, rolling stock, track, and facilities were in excess of what was required. Edward T. Reidy, CGW president, summed up the situation when he informed the ICC in 1965 that there was too much transportation service available between principal cities.

One solution was to consolidate railroads into fewer companies. CGW began to aggressively seek a partner during the early 1960s after management decided that a favorable merger was crucial to protect the interests of the company's shareholders. CGW and Chicago and North Western Railway (C&NW) began discussions in September 1964 on consolidating the two companies. They determined that a merger, with C&NW as the surviving company, would save $6 million per year through the elimination of duplicate track and facilities. It would also provide C&NW with access to Kansas City, a desire long held by that company. On November 13, 1964, the two railroads filed a petition with the ICC to approve their merger plans.

The regulatory process took three years to complete, and the ICC unanimously approved the merger on April 20, 1967. The decision, however, was appealed by the Soo Line, which sought protective conditions from traffic diversions caused by the consolidation. The ICC eventually imposed these conditions and issued a final reaffirmation of its decision on June 8, 1968.

On Monday, July 1, 1968, at 12:01 a.m., CGW ceased to exist as an independent company, and it became the C&NW Missouri Division. Both railroads had once served 44 points in common in four states, and much of the CGW was redundant. Most of the line was abandoned during the 1970s and 1980s, and only a few segments of former CGW right-of-way remain in operation. Elsewhere, it has been converted into other uses, including nature trails.

The objective of this book is to add more information to a limited historical record. Only a handful of books have been published about CGW and, on occasion, various historical journals or the railfan press will print an article about the railroad. The Chicago and North Western Historical Society has undertaken the task of preserving the history of CGW to a more extensive degree, including preservation of invaluable documents and maps, and there are a few railroad museums in the Midwest that maintain and display collections of CGW memorabilia.

The following chapters will take a look at CGW employees, locomotives, freight and passenger service, and the company's line in Illinois. Geographical coverage was limited to Illinois, although the company's history begins in Minnesota and most of its mileage was located in Iowa, because Illinois is the author's home state. He was partly raised near the CGW main line in Chicago and Bellwood, and a mix of memories and nostalgia has led to years of research about this interesting railroad and its operations in Illinois.

The chapter on locomotives covers the primary motive power operated, both steam and diesel-electric (called motors by CGW). Information on steam locomotives includes the Whyte system for wheel arrangement and name. The Whyte system shows the number of wheels starting at the front end with lead truck, drivers, and trailing truck. CGW engines were used throughout the Midwest, and most of the company's business consisted of interstate shipments and travel. Therefore, the chapters on motive power, freight service, and passenger service include coverage outside Illinois.

The chapter on the company's main line in Illinois begins in Chicago and heads west to Iowa. It was mainly a single-track route that passed through several counties, including Cook, DuPage, Kane, DeKalb, Ogle, a tip of Stephenson, and finally Jo Daviess. There were 49 CGW stations in Illinois by 1910, which included milk sheds and platforms at road crossings and are more than can be shown in the following pages. Instead, this book will look at the company's important terminals and a few smaller stations selected at random.

CGW published a directory of industries in January 1957 that listed businesses at its stations, including industries served by other railroads. Excerpts are included for the stations covered in this book. The directory included a yes or no column to show if the serving railroad switched cars for CGW. Also, some customers were shown as served by the local CGW team track. These companies picked up or delivered their shipments at CGW depot.

Chicago Great Western emblems

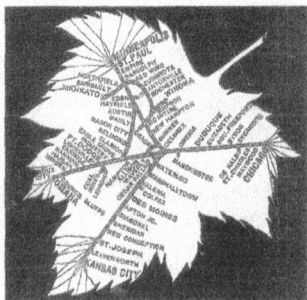

CGW used these various emblems over the years, which were printed on the covers of public timetables, advertisements, rolling stock, and locomotives. The maple leaf was in use from 1892 to 1910; the corn belt logo, in various formats, from 1910 to 1950; and the so-called "Lucky Strike" from 1950 to 1968. The emblem that features a steam locomotive was also used at various times during the 1920s and 1930s. (Author's collection.)

One

EMPLOYEES

This is the train crew assigned to switching service between Sycamore and DeKalb, Illinois, on July 9, 1949. The occasion was the run of the last CGW steam locomotive in Illinois. The engine was No. 467, nicknamed "The Goat." (Joiner History Room, Sycamore, Illinois.)

Famous people who worked for CGW included Walter P. Chrysler, the founder of Chrysler Corporation, and Frank B. Kellogg, secretary of state in the Coolidge administration. However, the majority were workers like the officials and crew of No. 436, who provided patrons with reliable and (usually) safe service. (Joiner History Room, Sycamore, Illinois.)

On June 27, 1962, fireman Robert Attwooll saved the life of a toddler at Hansell, Iowa. The child was standing too close to the track, and the engineer was unable to stop in time. Attwooll climbed onto the locomotive footboard and pushed the toddler clear. CGW published an article about Attwooll's heroism in the company newsletter, *Safety News*. (Author's collection.)

Two

LOCOMOTIVES

This track profile from the company's 1957 annual report displays ruling grades on CGW main lines. The choice of locomotive is partly based upon ruling grades, which is where the engine has to produce the most power to prevent a heavy train from stalling as it ascends upgrade. (Author's collection.)

CGW located its locomotive repair shops at Oelwein, Iowa, because it was centrally located. Oelwein shops were placed in service on September 28, 1899, and replaced a smaller facility at South Park, Minnesota. (Author's collection.)

GREAT WESTERN R R SHOPS, OELWEIN, IOWA.

Oelwein consisted of a storehouse and shops for erecting locomotives, fabricating boilers, and repairing and painting equipment. Walter P. Chrysler was employed at Oelwein as master mechanic in 1906 and was promoted to superintendent of motive power the following year. He remained with the CGW until 1909. (Author's collection.)

14

CGW operated a fleet of typical 19th-century motive power consisting of 4-4-0 American and 2-6-0 Mogul–type steam locomotives during the 1880s and 1890s. These engines were no longer suitable for requirements by 1901, and CGW began to acquire 2-6-2 Prairie and 2-8-0 Consolidation types as replacements. No. 180 was the first of 95 Prairies purchased from American Locomotive Company (ALCO) between 1902 and 1903. (Joiner History Room, Sycamore, Illinois.)

No. 289 was one of the Prairies purchased from ALCO in 1903. This photograph shows its appearance years later. Twenty-three Prairies were assigned to passenger service, and the remainder was used to power freight trains. CGW owned more Prairies than any other type of steam locomotive. (Joiner History Room, Sycamore, Illinois.)

The 2-8-0 Consolidation type was the workhorse on almost all railroads in the United States between 1866 and 1916. CGW acquired a total of 60 from Baldwin Locomotive Works and Rhode Island Locomotive Works between 1900 and 1910. The Consolidations were used to power heavy freight trains, especially between Chicago and Oelwein. The main line west of Stockton, Illinois, consisted of steep grades, which necessitated the use of powerful locomotives. No. 340 was purchased from Baldwin in 1910. (Author's collection.)

Consolidation No. 349 was also acquired from Baldwin in 1910. CGW upgraded its Consolidations over the years, and many of the locomotives survived until 1950, although out of service by that time. The Consolidations were used as switchers when replaced with more powerful locomotives. (Author's collection.)

16

LOCOMOTIVE RATING IN TONS OF 2,000 POUNDS BETWEEN TENDER AND CABOOSE.								
Engine Numbers	300 to 319	220 to 292	180 to 219	900 150 to 920 175	100 to 148	90 to 95	70 to 85	15 to 69
Percentage D. B. Pull	132	110	100	83	65	60	50	44
EAST-BOUND.								
Dyersville to Farley ... 6 miles	1450	1200	1075	925	750	675	560	490
Galena Junction to Stockton ... 26 miles	1200	1000	900	750	600	550	450	390
Oelwein to Chicago with helpers on above grades ... 245 miles	1900	1600	1400	1250	1000	925	750	650
WEST-BOUND.								
Rodden to Winston ... 2 miles / Kidder to Farley ... 4 miles	1200	1000	900	750	600	550	450	390
Chicago to Oelwein with helpers on above grades ... 245 miles	1500	1250	1100	950	775	700	575	500

LIGHT WEIGHTS.

40,000 lb. flats and gondolas	10 tons	Baggage cars, ... hand derrick cars	25 tons
70,000 lb. flats or 40,000 lb. box	12 "	8 wheel coaches and sleeping cars	30 "
70,000 lb. gondolas, 50,000 lb. box cabooses	13 "	12 wheel coaches and sleeping cars	40 "
Stock cars ... 60,000 lb. box, tank cars	15 "	Mogul engine and tender	70 "
46 ft. furniture ... 70,000 lb. box	17 "	Steam derrick cars	80 "
50 ft. furniture ... refrigerator	19 "	Heavier engine and tender	110 "
Engine tender ... 80,000 lb. box	20 "		

This locomotive rating chart was published in Eastern Division employee timetable No. 20, effective August 8, 1909. Note Consolidations, Nos. 300 to 319, could haul more tonnage than Prairies, Nos. 180 to 292. CGW had not yet purchased the remainder of its Consolidations, including Nos. 340 and 349, when the chart was prepared. (Chicago and North Western Historical Society.)

CGW published this list of locomotives in the company's 1911 annual report. The motive power fleet consisted of 318 steam engines and four motorcars as of June 30, 1911. The motorcars were combination passenger-mail-express vehicles fueled by gasoline. (Author's collection.)

CHICAGO GREAT WESTERN RAILROAD COMPANY

EXHIBIT 23

LOCOMOTIVES OWNED AND CHANGES, YEAR ENDED JUNE 30, 1911

	Wheel Arrangement	Owned June 30, 1910	Added by purchase during the Year	Sold, Broken up or Condemned	Changed from another Class	Changed to another Class	Owned June 30, 1911
SWITCHING:							
Cylinders, 16 x 24	00	4		4			0
SWITCHING:							
Cylinders, 17 x 24	000	8		2			6
Cylinders, 18 x 24		8		3			5
Cylinders, 19 x 26		5					5
Cylinders, 20 x 26			10				10
SWITCHING:							
Cylinders, 20½ x 30	0000				1		1
Cylinders, 22 x 32		6			4		10
TOTAL SWITCHING		31	10	9	5		37
TRANSFER:							
Cylinders, 20½ x 30	000o	10		2		8	0
EIGHT-WHEEL:							
Cylinders, 17 x 24	00oo	37		6			31
Cylinders, 18 x 24		12		2			10
Cylinders, 19 x 24		9					9
TOTAL EIGHT-WHEEL		58		8			50
MOGUL:							
Cylinders, 18 x 24	000o	35		5			30
Cylinders, 19 x 28		2					2
Cylinders, 19 x 24		12		2			10
MOGUL CROSS COMPOUND:							
Cylinders, 21 and 22 x 24	000o	2		2			0
TOTAL MOGUL		51		9			42
TEN-WHEEL:							
Cylinders, 18 x 26	000oo	2					2
Cylinders, 19 x 26		4					4
Cylinders, 20 x 28		14			7		21
Cylinders, 26 x 28		4					4
Cylinders, 23 x 28			6				6
TEN-WHEEL CROSS COMPOUND:							
Cylinders, 22 and 35 x 28	000oo	7				7	0
TOTAL TEN-WHEEL		31	6		7	7	37
PRAIRIE:							
Cylinders, 20 x 26	o000o	15			6		9
Cylinders, 21 x 26		3					3
Cylinders, 21 x 28		26			4	3	27
Cylinders, 24 x 28		12			17		29
PRAIRIE CROSS COMPOUND:							
Cylinders, 22 and 35 x 28	o000o	14				14	0
PRAIRIE TANDEM COMPOUND:							
Cylinders, 16 and 26 x 28	o000o	20				7	13
TOTAL PRAIRIE		90			21	30	81
CONSOLIDATION:							
Cylinders, 24 x 30	000o	20	20				40
Cylinders, 20½ x 30						7	7
CONSOLIDATION CROSS COMPOUND:							
Cylinders, 22 and 35 x 32	000oo	4			4		0
TOTAL CONSOLIDATION		24	20		7	4	47
PACIFIC:							
Cylinders, 20 x 26	o000oo	3			3		6
Cylinders, 24 x 26		3			3		5
TOTAL PACIFIC		5			6		11
MALLET COMPOUND:							
Cylinders, 22 and 35 x 32	o0000oo	0	10				10
Cylinders, 21 and 35 x 28		0			3		3
TOTAL MALLET		0	10		3		13
GRAND TOTAL		300	46	28	49	49	318
MOTOR CARS		0	4				4
TOTAL MOTOR CARS		0	4				4

38

The Mallet 2-6-6-2 articulated locomotive was developed during the early 1900s for moving heavy tonnage over steep grades. CGW acquired 10 in 1910 from Baldwin for service between Stockton and Oelwein. The plan was to use Consolidations between Chicago and Stockton and Mallets between Stockton and Oelwein. Previously, train size was reduced west of Stockton if powered with a Consolidation or the company-assigned helper engines. The Mallet was powerful enough to pull the same train without reducing size or dispatching helpers. However, the Mallets were too slow and expensive to operate and maintain. All 10 were sold to the Clinchfield Railroad in 1916. No. 603, shown at Oelwein in 1912, was one of these behemoths. (James L. Rueber.)

In 1910, CGW also built three Mallets at Oelwein from Prairies by attaching new Baldwin boilers and engines to the front end. Note the circular connection joint at the middle of the boiler. The homebuilt Mallets shared the same problems that affected the Baldwin engines and also were unable to produce enough steam while in operation. CGW converted the three into 4-6-2 Pacific types in 1915. (James L. Rueber.)

18

When the Mallet failed to meet expectations, CGW turned to the 2-8-2 Mikado type for moving heavy tonnage. The Mikado could haul more than the Consolidation, but the grades west of Stockton forced the CGW to resume reducing tonnage or assigning helper engines. CGW purchased 40 Mikados from Baldwin between 1912 and 1920. No. 729 was photographed at Oelwein in November 1934. (Author's collection.)

The versatility of the Mikado type to power either freight or passenger trains is shown in this photograph of No. 740 at Sycamore, Illinois. No. 740 was one of several Mikados rebuilt by CGW between 1937 and 1939 with automatic stokers, new frames, and disc-type main drivers. (Joiner History Room, Sycamore, Illinois.)

NEW LOCOMOTIVES SHOW
EFFICIENCY

Consolidation Type Locomotive, Chicago Great Western Ry.

A recent test of twelve months duration, carried out on the Chicago Great Western Railway, illustrates the economies realized by using high power locomotives of modern design. This test was run on the Eastern Division where the maximum grades are one per cent. The locomotives tested included ten of the Consolidation type, built by The Baldwin Locomotive Works in 1909, and ten of the Mikado type, completed by the same builders in 1912. The former use saturated steam, while the latter are equipped with superheaters. The average train load hauled by the Mikado type engines was 53 per cent. greater than that hauled by the Consolidations, and this was done with a saving, on a ton-mile basis, of 37 per cent. in pounds of coal consumed, and 38 per cent. in cost of maintenance.

In this case the motive power was specially fitted for the work to be done. Similar results can be obtained on other roads, provided equal care is taken in selecting the locomotives. The Chicago Great Western test demonstrates the remarkable progress made in locomotive efficiency during the past few years.

Mikado Type Locomotive, Chicago Great Western Ry.
G. M. Crownover, Supt. Motive Power.

THE BALDWIN LOCOMOTIVE WORKS
PHILADELPHIA, PA., U. S. A.

Represented by

F. W. Weston, 50 Church Street, New York, N. Y.   Charles Riddell, 625 Railway Exchange, Chicago, Ill.
C. H. Peterson, 1610 Wright Building, St. Louis, Mo.   A. Wm. Hinger, 722 Spalding Building, Portland, Ore.
George F. Jones, 407 Travelers Building, Richmond, Va.
Cable Address: "BALDWIN, PHILADELPHIA."

CGW frequently conducted comparison trials between locomotives to determine if it was using the most efficient engine. This 1915 Baldwin advertisement reported on the better performance of the Mikado than the Consolidation in freight service between Chicago and Oelwein. (Author's collection.)

The 2-10-4 Texas–type locomotive was first built in 1925 for the Texas and Pacific Railway for hauling heavy tonnage at high speed over long distances. CGW found that the Texas had 30 percent more hauling capacity than the Mikado, with lower maintenance cost. Between 1929 and 1930, 36 were purchased from Lima Locomotive Works and Baldwin. The first Texas purchased from Baldwin, No. 800, was photographed at St. Paul, Minnesota, on July 18, 1947. (Author's collection.)

The Texas replaced the Mikado in heavy tonnage freight service between Chicago and St. Paul and between Oelwein and Kirmeyer, Missouri. The 2-10-4 produced enough power to pull freight trains over the steep grades west of Stockton with no reduction in train size or helpers. No. 850, the first CGW Texas built by Lima, was photographed at Chicago Transfer Yard on October 15, 1939. (James L. Rueber.)

Locomotives assigned to switching service performed the highly important work of breakdown and makeup of trains in classification yards and pickup and delivery of freight cars at industries and interchanges. ALCO built No. 450, a 0-6-0 switcher, in 1902. (Joiner History Room, Sycamore, Illinois.)

Switching is very demanding work for train crews and locomotives due to constant starting, stopping, and reversal of movement. Switcher No. 482 was photographed at Chicago Transfer Yard in 1937. (Joiner History Room, Sycamore, Illinois.)

CGW acquired 37 4-6-0 Ten Wheelers from Baldwin, Lima, Rhode Island, and Richmond Locomotive Works between 1899 and 1910. The engines were assigned to power the company's premier passenger trains, including the Great Western Limited, which ran between Chicago and Minneapolis–St. Paul. No. 503 was painted dark green and black, and most of the external piping on the boiler was hidden under an outer casing for a streamlined appearance. (Joiner History Room, Sycamore, Illinois.)

Ten Wheeler No. 507 was built by Baldwin in October 1910 and had provided 39 years of service when photographed at Oelwein on March 20, 1949. The worn condition of CGW steam locomotives by the late 1940s is apparent. (Author's collection.)

The 4-6-2 Pacific was also used to power passenger trains on the CGW, which had a fleet of 38. Eight were purchased from Baldwin in 1913 and 1916, and the remainder was built at Oelwein by modifying 2-6-2 Prairies and the homebuilt Mallets. No. 914 began as a Prairie type, rebuilt in 1916 and further modernized in 1923. The photograph was taken at St. Paul, Minnesota, on May 29, 1948. (Author's collection.)

No. 932 was the last of the eight Pacific-type engines acquired from Baldwin. These locomotives were the most powerful 4-6-2s operated by CGW and were assigned to the fastest and heaviest passenger trains. (Author's collection.)

The CGW steam locomotive fleet was in need of replacement after World War II, when railroads were converting their motive power from steam to the more efficient diesel-electric. Electro-Motive Division (EMD) of General Motors provided CGW with diesel model F-3 No. 291 for test purposes during November 1946, and the railroad quickly became aware of the potential savings offered by this type of power. CGW ordered its first diesels on December 19, 1946, and began to retire its steam engines. This photograph shows "dead" steam locomotives passing through Richardson, Illinois, en route to Oelwein for sale to scrap dealers. (Joiner History Room, Sycamore, Illinois.)

CGW began to power freight trains in Illinois with diesels on October 11, 1947. Steam locomotives were limited to switching service and local wayfreight, and motorcars powered passenger trains. The last active CGW steam locomotive in Illinois, No. 467, completed its final trip on July 9, 1949, and at that time, all CGW motive power in the Prairie State was diesel-electric. Later, in 1951, CGW dismantled all of the water tanks and coal chutes in Illinois that were previously used for steam engines. Oelwein became a steam locomotive graveyard as CGW completed the conversion of its motive power. (Author's collection.)

CGW purchased four McKeen Motor Car Company railcars in 1910 and the first Electro-Motive Company gas-electric car in 1924. The railcars were less expensive to operate than steam locomotives and were used to handle passenger business on lightly patronized lines. The CGW railcar fleet eventually totaled 16 vehicles. M-1009 was one of four purchased from Pullman Car and Manufacturing Company in 1932. It was a 450-horsepower combination mail-express-passenger coach with seating capacity for 22 passengers. The Pullmans were assigned to local passenger trains that operated between Chicago and Oelwein. The first railcar placed in this service made the maiden voyage on April 1, 1932. (Joiner History Room, Sycamore, Illinois.)

CGW purchased a gasoline-powered switcher from Baldwin in 1925 and assigned it No. 1. The company acquired its first diesel-electric locomotive from Westinghouse Electric and Manufacturing Company for yard switching at Oelwein in 1934 and designated it No. 2. It was placed on public display at Grand Central Station, Chicago, during December 1934. Two more diesel-electric switchers, Nos. 3 and 4, were also acquired from Westinghouse in April 1936. All four were rated at 800 horsepower. This is a photograph of No. 4 at Oelwein. (James L. Rueber.)

The diesel-electric locomotive was first developed to replace steam locomotives in switching service because it provides full power immediately and consumes less fuel when stopped and idling. A steam locomotive does not have these capabilities. The first CGW diesels were acquired for switching work and included No. 10, one of three model S-2 1,000-horsepower units purchased from ALCO in 1947. The locomotive has derailed, and the train crew is waiting for assistance. (Joiner History Room, Sycamore, Illinois.)

Here is No. 10 again but in better circumstances. Note the different CGW emblem on the cab side. This photograph was taken on February 25, 1967, at Chicago Transfer Yard. (Joseph Piersen.)

No. 34 is one of 10 Baldwin model DS-4-4-1000, 1,000-horsepower engines acquired in 1949 for switching service. It was photographed on May 28, 1968, at St. Paul. CGW became completely dieselized in September 1949 and was the first railroad in its territory to achieve this status. (Author's collection.)

The 10 Baldwin DS-4-4-1000 switchers also included No. 38. CGW reported to the Association of American Railroads on January 1, 1950, that it owned 137 diesel-electric locomotives at that time, which represented 87 percent of its motive power fleet. (Author's collection.)

This information on CGW diesel-electric locomotives was published in employee timetable No. 3, effective October 1, 1965. The Cooper's Rating table was used to determine if a bridge was designed to support the weight of a particular locomotive. Diesels with boilers were assigned to passenger trains because the boiler provided heating. (Author's collection.)

CLASSIFICATION OF LOCOMOTIVES

Class	Units	Locomotive Numbers
D-1	1	2
D-2	6	6, 11, 12, 13, 14, 15
D-3	31	5, 8, 9, 10 and 16 to 42, inc.
D-4	18	58 A-B to 66 A-B, inc.
D-5	8	50 to 57, inc.
D-6	2	120-121
D-7	4	101 A-B-C-D
"	2	102 B-D
"	3	103 A-B-D
"	3	104 A-B-D
"	2	105 B-D
"	4	106 A-B-C-D
"	4	107 A-B-C-D
"	4	108 A-B-C-D
"	4	109 A-B-C-D
"	4	110 A-B-C-D
"	4	111 A-B-C-D
"	4	112 A-B-C-D
"	4	113 A-B-C-D
"	4	114 A-B-C-D
"	4	115 A-B-C-D
"	7	116 A-B-C-D-E-F-G
"	5	150, 152, 153, 155, 156
D-8	8	201 to 208 inc.
Total.........	140	

COOPER'S RATING OF C.G.W. LOCOMOTIVES

D-1 .... E-47
D-2 .... E-40
D-3 .... E-49
D-4 .... E-49
D-5 .... E-46
D-6 .... E-50
D-7 .... E-47
D-8 .... E-57

Diesel Units Equipped With Steam Boilers

114-B	115-B	115-D	116-A	116-B	116-C
116-D	116-E	116-F	116-G	150	
152	153		155	156	

Diesel Units Equipped With Steam Connections But No Boilers

102-D	104-D	112-D	113-B	113-D	114-D
		120	121		

CGW purchased 18 model TR-2 engines from General Motors' EMD in 1948 and 1949. The designation TR referred to transfer service, which is moving trains from one railroad to another within yard limits. The engine was connected to a booster unit that provided extra power. The configuration was nicknamed "cow and calf." No. 59 and its calf were photographed at Oelwein on April 26, 1962. (James L. Rueber.)

The cab-type diesel-electric symbolized the CGW motive power fleet as it existed between 1949 and 1968. All of the cab types were purchased from EMD between 1947 and 1951, primarily for freight service. The diesel-electric permitted CGW to achieve efficiency by powering trains with fewer locomotives. (Author's collection.)

A typical, long CGW freight train powered by four cab-type diesels was photographed crossing the Des Moines River Valley Bridge at Fort Dodge, Iowa. EMD estimated the diesel-electric locomotive would return 17.2 percent annually in savings on the investment in new power. William Deramus III, CGW president, informed shareholders in 1950 that the return exceeded expectations and was 30 percent. (James L. Rueber.)

CGW acquired two model GP-7 (general purpose) diesels from EMD in 1951 for wayfreight service, including No. 120. This particular engine was almost destroyed in a fire at the Forty-sixth Street roundhouse near Chicago Transfer Yard on September 15, 1955. It was rebuilt the following year as an updated version designated GP-9. The photograph was taken on September 5, 1965, at Chicago Transfer Yard. (James L. Rueber.)

Here is GP-7 No. 121. The units were referred to as "jeeps" (GP) and were just as rugged and reliable. Nos. 120 and 121 are the author's favorite CGW motive power. No. 121 was photographed at Chicago Transfer Yard on July 17, 1966. (Author's collection.)

CGW completed its initial acquisition of diesel-electric locomotives in 1951, and at that time, the fleet consisted of 102 road locomotives, 39 switchers, and two railcars. The next purchase of diesels occurred in 1963, when CGW acquired model GP-30 locomotives from EMD. A drawing of the first unit, No. 201, was featured on the cover of the company's 1963 annual report. (Author's collection.)

Two of eight new Electro-Motive GP-30 diesel locomotive units acquired and placed in service in August, 1963.

The GP-30 produced more power than the older cab units and allowed the CGW to assign fewer engines to a heavy tonnage train. For example, six cab units coupled together produced 9,000 horsepower, which was the same as four GP-30s coupled together. An article in the September and October 1963 issue of *Safety News* reported that the new GP-30s made a distinctive sound when running, and the sound of the air horn chime was also unique. (Author's collection.)

Compare the photograph of GP-30 No. 208 when new with this picture of the same unit three years later. Wear and tear and faded paint are the result of continual operation pulling heavy tonnage trains day after day through all types of weather. This photograph of No. 208 was taken at Kansas City, Missouri, on May 28, 1966. (Author's collection.)

CGW purchased its last motive power in 1966, when it acquired 10 model SD-40 (special duty) locomotives built by EMD. The SD-40s were rated at 3,000 horsepower each. No. 402 was photographed at C&NW shops in Minneapolis in July 1968. (Author's collection.)

The SD-40 type was the first CGW diesel to be equipped with six-wheel trucks, and the company described the engines as the finest in modern motive power. No. 405 was also photographed at the C&NW Minneapolis shops in July 1968. (Author's collection.)

Three

FREIGHT SERVICE

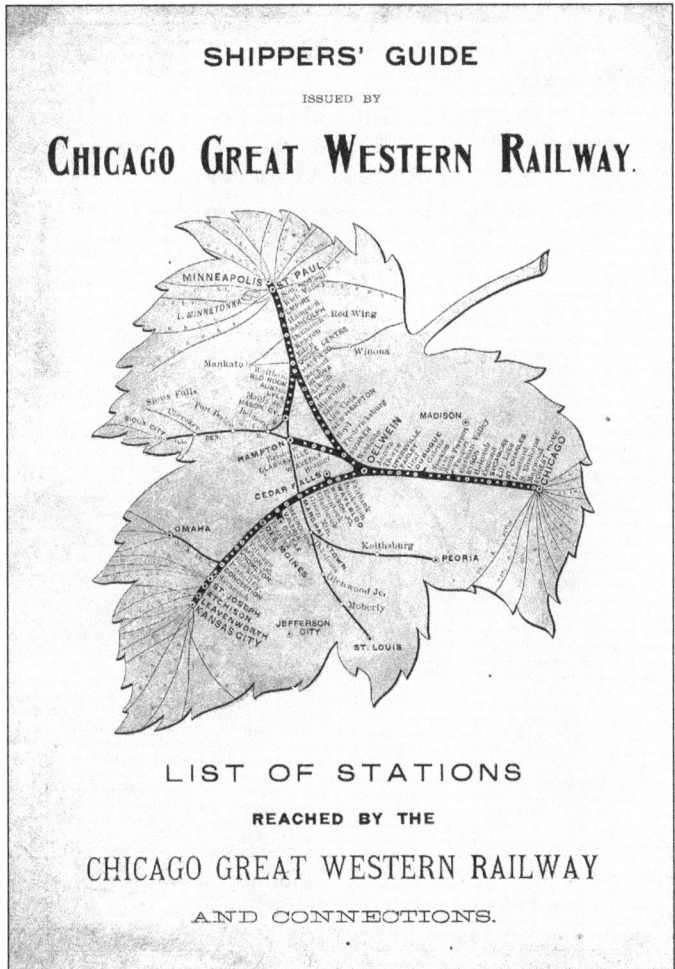

This is a CGW shippers' guide published during the 1890s. The guide contained a list of stations served by CGW and connecting railroads. Note the maple leaf trademark. Predecessor company CStP&KC conducted a nationwide trademark contest among ticket agents in 1889, and the winning submission was a sugar maple leaf that depicted the company's lines as veins on the leaf. The winner of the contest was a Wabash Railroad employee who received a prize of $100 for his entry. (Author's collection.)

The station agent and his helper are loading milk and express in the baggage car of an eastbound train at Byron, Illinois. This scene was repeated frequently at stations all along the CGW system over the years. (Byron Museum of History.)

Railroad freight service includes switching cars at industries and interchanges. Switcher No. 482 is pushing a freight car across a grade crossing. Note the engineer leaning out the cab window, watching for hand signals from his brakeman. Also note the absence of crossing gates or flagmen. (Joiner History Room, Sycamore, Illinois.)

The crew of locomotive No. 263 appears to be ready to back a freight car onto another track, or else something of interest has caught their attention. The photograph was taken at Minneapolis, and the weather must have been warm. The ventilators on the cab roof are opened as well as the cab door. (Author's collection.)

CGW operated a complex system of freight activities, including switching at industries and interchanges, moving freight trains between terminals, and classifying freight cars in yards at Oelwein, Chicago, Minneapolis, St. Paul, Omaha, and Kansas City. Locomotive No. 270 was photographed switching an industry siding. (Author's collection.)

Railroads publish freight rates in schedules such as CGW tariff No. 15-B, which contained charges on shipping brick, drain tile, and stone. Increases, decreases, and other revisions were published in supplements. (Author's collection.)

CGW published a revised rate schedule on shipping brick between Chicago and other Illinois stations in supplement No. 41 to tariff 15-B, effective July 21, 1919. The list of stations indicates no agent at West St. Charles, Lovell's Crossing, Five Points, Bruceville, Winston, Rice, and Aiken. Therefore, charges had to be prepaid when shipping to these points. (Author's collection.)

This is a 1914 advertisement on CGW fast freight service. Railroads had to offer this type of service to meet shipper demands. For example, in 1911, the railroads lengthened transit times between Chicago and western cities from second-morning delivery to third after the ICC refused to allow an increase in freight rates. Chicago merchants and produce dealers quickly lodged a strenuous protest and vowed to boycott any road that failed to resume second-morning service. The railroads held firm, but their resolve ended several months later when CGW decided to comply with shipper demands and reinstated second-morning service. (Author's collection.)

THROUGH FAST FREIGHT SERVICE

BETWEEN NORTH AND SOUTH

NORTHBOUND
Leave KANSAS CITY..........6.25 P.M.
Arrive ST. PAUL...............7.00 A.M.
Arrive MINNEAPOLIS........11.00 A.M.
Time in transit—
To St. Paul, 36 hours, 35 minutes.
To Minneapolis, 40 hours, 35 minutes.

SOUTHBOUND
Leave MINNEAPOLIS..........6.00 P.M.
Leave ST. PAUL................11.00 P.M.
Arrive KANSAS CITY.........5.20 A.M.
Time in transit—
From Minneapolis, 59 hours, 20 minutes.
From St. Paul, 54 hours, 20 minutes.

These expedited through trains offer unexcelled service for the handling of perishable freight and other commodities in both carload and less than carload quantities, between points in the South and Southwest and points in Minnesota, the Dakotas, Montana, North Pacific Coast States and the Canadian Northwest. The exchange of commodities between these sections is rapidly increasing, and the needs of this traffic for a prompt through service have been anticipated by this Company in the arrangement of its schedules between the southwest Missouri River Crossings and the Twin Cities.

BETWEEN EAST AND WEST

Fast freight trains are operated daily in both directions between Chicago and the Missouri River and the Twin Cities, handling carload and less than carload traffic.

WESTBOUND: Trains depart from Chicago at 7.00 P. M., arriving St. Joseph at 6.30 A. M., Leavenworth 11.30 A. M., Kansas City 2.00 P. M., Council Bluffs 4.30 P. M., and St. Paul 2.00 P. M. of the second day. Deliveries in Omaha and Minneapolis are made immediately following arrival of trains at Council Bluffs and St. Paul respectively.

EASTBOUND: Trains leave Kansas City at 6.25 P.M., Leavenworth 8.15 P.M., St. Joseph 10.50 P.M., Council Bluffs 9.00 P. M., and St. Paul 11.00 P.M., reaching Chicago 6.00 A.M. of the second day.

Close connections are made at Chicago with lines operating to the East, Southeast and South, and at the Missouri River and St. Paul with lines operating in all directions, insuring the prompt interchange of through traffic and its expeditious movement.

Details concerning service, rates or other information will be furnished by any of the Company's representatives whose names and addresses appear on page 4, or by

OSCAR TOWNSEND, General Freight Agent,
1129 Peoples Gas Building,
CHICAGO, ILL.

FREIGHT SCHEDULES

From Chicago

Stations		Time	Day		Time	Day
Chicago	Lv 143	7 00	0	Lv 91	11 00	0
Bellwood	Lv 143	7 55	0	Lv 91	12 15	1
Ingalton	Lv 143	8 40	0	Lv 91	1 00	1
Sycamore	Lv 143	9 35	0	Lv 91	2 00	1
South Freeport	Lv 143	11 30	0	Lv 91	3 35	1
Galena Junction	Lv 143	1 15	0	Lv 91	5 15	1
Dubuque	Lv 143	1 45	0	Lv 91	8 45	1
Oelwein	An 143	4 15	0	An 91	9 15	1
Oelwein	Lv 42	6 00	0	Lv 92	8 50	1
McIntire	Lv 42	9 20	0	Lv 92	11 15	1
Hayfield	Lv 42	11 15	0	Lv 92	1 00	1
Randolph	An 42	1 45	1	An 92	3 15	1
South Saint Paul	An 42	2 45	1	An 92	4 25	1
Saint Paul	An 42	3 00	1	An 92	4 45	1
Oelwein	Lv 43	8 00	0	Lv 41	11 00	1
Waterloo	An 43	9 30	0	An 41	12 45	1
Marshalltown	An 43	11 20	0	An 41	2 55	1
Des Moines	An 43	2 20	1	An 41	5 15	1
Des Moines	Lv 43	3 20	1	Lv 41	6 15	1
Conception	An 43	8 00	1	An 41	11 20	1
Saint Joseph	An 43	10 10	1	An 41	12 30	2
Kansas City	An 43	2 00	1	An 41	4 00	2
Oelwein	Lv 91	4 00	1			
Waverly	Lv 91	5 10	1			
Hampton	Lv 91	6 50	1			
Clarion	An 91	8 10	1			
Fort Dodge	An 91	9 05	1			
Council Bluffs	An 91	2 00	1			

From Minneapolis-St. Paul

Stations		Time	Day		Time	Day
St. Paul	Lv 43	6 00	0	Lv 41	4 45	0
So. St. Paul	Lv 43	6 30	0	Lv 41	5 30	0
Randolph	Lv 43	8 15	0	Lv 41	7 01	0
Hayfield	Lv 43	11 00	0	Lv 41	8 55	0
McIntire	Lv 43	12 15	0	Lv 41	10 40	0
Oelwein	An 43	3 00	0	An 41	1 00	1
Oelwein	Lv 90	4 00	0	Lv 192	2 00	1
Dubuque	An 90	7 05	0	An 192	6 15	1
Galena Jct.	Lv 90	7 35	0	Lv 192	6 45	1
So. Freeport	Lv 90	9 40	0	Lv 192	8 40	1
Sycamore	Lv 90	11 20	0	Lv 192	10 13	1
Ingalton	An 90	12 10	1	An 192	11 10	1
Bellwood	An 90	1 00	1	An 192	12 10	1
Chicago	An 90	1 45	1	An 192	1 00	1
Oelwein	An 43	8 00	0	Lv 41	11 00	1
Waterloo	An 43	9 30	0	An 41	12 45	1
Marshalltown a	Lv 43	12 01	1	An 41	2 55	1
Des Moines	An 43	5 15	1	An 41	5 15	1
Des Moines	Lv 48	3 20	1	Lv 41	6 15	1
Conception	An 43	8 10	1	An 41	11 20	1
St. Joseph	An 43	10 10	1	An 41	12 30	2
Kansas City	An 43	2 00	1	An 41	4 00	2
Oelwein	An 91	4 00	0			
Waverly	An 91	5 10	0			
Hampton	Lv 91	6 50	0			
Clarion	An 91	8 10	0			
Fort Dodge	An 91	9 05	0			
Council Bluffs	An 91	2 00	1			

From Kansas City

Stations		Time	Day		Time	Day
Kansas City	Lv 92	7 00	0	Lv 42	7 00	0
St. Joseph	Lv 92	10 10	0	Lv 42	10 30	0
Conception	Lv 92	11 45	0	Lv 42	12 15	1
Des Moines	An 92	3 45	0	An 42	4 20	1
Des Moines	Lv 92	5 30	0	Lv 42	5 15	1
Marshalltown	An 92	8 20	0	An 42	8 15	1
Waterloo	An 92	11 00	0	An 42	10 45	1
Oelwein	An 92	12 15	1	An 42	11 59	1
Oelwein	Lv 92	8 30	1	Lv 42	6 00	1
McIntire	Lv 92	11 15	1	Lv 42	9 20	1
Hayfield	Lv 92	1 00	1	Lv 42	11 15	1
Randolph	An 92	3 15	1	An 42	1 45	2
So. St. Paul	An 92	4 28	1	An 42	2 45	2
St. Paul	An 92	4 45	1	An 42	3 00	2
Oelwein	Lv 192	2 00	1	An 90	4 00	1
Dubuque	An 192	6 15	1	An 90	7 05	1
Galena Jct.	Lv 192	6 45	1	Lv 90	7 35	1
So. Freeport	Lv 192	8 40	1	Lv 90	9 40	1
Sycamore	Lv 192	10 13	1	Lv 90	11 20	1
Ingalton	An 192	11 10	1	An 90	12 10	2
Bellwood	An 192	12 10	1	An 90	1 00	2
Chicago	An 192	1 00	1	An 90	1 45	2
Oelwein	Lv 91	4 00	1			
Waverly	Lv 91	5 10	1			
Hampton	Lv 91	6 50	1			
Clarion	An 91	8 10	1			
Fort Dodge	An 91	9 05	1			
Council Bluffs	An 91	2 00	2			

SHIP VIA CHICAGO GREAT WESTERN RAILWAY

A.M. Figures Light

P.M. Figures Dark

Further details may be secured from traffic representatives listed herein.

From Omaha-Council Bluffs

Stations		Time	Day
Council Bluffs	Lv 90	7 00	0
Fort Dodge	An 90	12 00	0
Clarion	An 90	12 55	0
Hampton	An 90	1 55	0
Waverly	An 90	3 25	0
Oelwein	An 90	4 00	0
Oelwein	Lv 90	4 00	0
Dubuque	An 90	7 05	0
Galena Jct.	Lv 90	7 35	0
So. Freeport	Lv 90	9 40	0
Sycamore	An 90	11 20	0
Ingalton	An 90	12 10	1
Bellwood	An 90	1 45	1
Oelwein	Lv 42	6 00	0
McIntire	Lv 42	9 20	0
Hayfield	Lv 42	11 15	0
Randolph	An 42	2 45	1
So. St. Paul	An 42	3 00	1
St. Paul	An 42	3 00	1
Oelwein	Lv 43	8 00	0
Marshalltown	An 43	12 01	1
Des Moines	An 43	3 20	1
Des Moines	Lv 43	3 20	1
Conception	An 43	8 00	1
St. Joseph	An 43	10 10	1
Kansas City	An 43	2 00	1

Shown is a CGW freight schedule effective April 27, 1952. The company completed an extensive rehabilitation program during the early 1950s to modernize freight operations in conjunction with dieselization. The capacity of the classification yard at Oelwein was increased to 3,000 cars when rebuilt in 1952. (Author's collection.)

Ink blotters were used years ago to absorb excess ink from pens. Many companies used them as a form of advertising, such as this particular blotter provided to CGW patrons as a reminder that the company was "At Your Service." (Author's collection.)

The 2-8-0 Consolidation No. 355, in service as a switcher, was photographed shoving a tank car onto a siding. Spotting cars at industries and interchanges required skill and careful handling. Sometimes other cars had to be moved out of the way in order to get to one car. Also, industry sidings were not always well maintained, and it was not unusual to end up derailing a car while moving it along an old rusty spur track. (Author's collection.)

This list of junction points was published in 1914 to show travelers where they could make connections with other railroads. The information was also useful to identify track connections with other railroads for the interchange of freight cars. (Author's collection.)

Interchange connections with other roads is vital because 75 percent of rail shipments involve at least two railroads. CGW published this list of junctions and connecting railroads in 1952. The company also relied upon intermediate switching roads to complete connections, such as the Indiana Harbor Belt Railroad at Bellwood, Illinois, which facilitated interchange between CGW and 26 other railroads in Chicago. (Author's collection.)

Junction Points and Track Connections

CHICAGO GREAT WESTERN RAILWAY

ALPHABETICAL LIST OF JUNCTIONS AT WHICH

FREIGHT TRAFFIC

MAY BE DIRECTLY INTERCHANGED WITH CONNECTING LINES (Except as noted)

An eastbound CGW freight train powered by locomotive No. 860 is rushing past the depot at Wilkinson, Illinois, in 1935. Note the semitrailers on flatcars behind the tender. CGW was a pioneer in providing shippers with TOFC, or trailer-on-flatcar service, also referred to as "piggyback." (Joiner History Room, Sycamore, Illinois.)

YOUR Opportunity!

CHOOSING a location for your factory is no longer a question of momentary consideration. It is a question of scientific research. The accessibility to raw material markets, the labor supply, cost of fuel and power, living conditions, comparative freight rates and transportation service should all be considered.

Many a factory has failed because it was not advantageously located. Our highly efficient Industrial Department is at your service. We will gladly assist you and give you much valuable advice regarding these vital factors.

Write to-day. It will cost you nothing and may be the means of your saving thousands of dollars.

T. A. HOVERSTAD, *Development Agent*
CHICAGO GREAT WESTERN RAILROAD
Room 540, 29 So. La Salle St., Chicago, Ill.

CGW established an industrial department to develop online freight business, as shown in this 1921 advertisement. Aggressive solicitation efforts resulted in hundreds of large and small businesses locating warehouses, factories, lumberyards, and bulk oil storage facilities along the CGW. (Author's collection.)

The company promoted the operation of fast freight trains and terminal facilities as incentives to ship by the CGW. Freight facilities included team tracks and warehouses at terminals and stations for receipt and delivery of shipments. (Author's collection.)

High Geared to Speed the Nation's Traffic

Day after day Great Western scheduled fast freights speed the products of farm and industry regularly and dependably "on time" to America's markets.

The modern freight facilities of the Chicago Great Western Railway are geared to the Nation's traffic needs.

Your nearest Great Western Representative will be glad to tell how you can use the facilities of this railway to advantage.

G. R. GREGG, General Traffic Manager
309 West Jackson Boulevard
Chicago 6, Illinois

Traffic Offices in most of the larger Cities (See pages 3-6)

Chicago Great Western Railway
The Corn Belt Route

Locomotive No. 865, with engineer Herb Brown at the throttle, roars through Lombard, Illinois, with an eastbound freight train on November 7, 1940. CGW transported 6,069,807 tons of freight in 1940. (James L. Rueber.)

HAULING MORE
For Less

CHICAGO GREAT WESTERN
CORN BELT ROUTE
RAILWAY COMPANY

WE hear much about achievements these days. The American railroads are able to play their part and to meet the constantly increasing demands upon them because of the vast expenditures made during recent years in the rebuilding and improvement of their plant and facilities. When war came railroads were ready.

The Chicago Great Western Railway is proud of its place as a part of the great system of American railroads.

Not only that, but the Chicago Great Western Railway in 1942 received an average of only 0.847 cents for every ton of freight carried one mile — the lowest return for any year since 1918.

Completely rebuilt for faster freight service, powered with huge locomotives of the 2-10-4 type, and with its track and equipment maintained to a high standard, the Chicago Great Western Railway serves the Nation's war effort and the varied industry and commerce that centers in the Heart of America.

The company transported the highest volume of freight traffic in its history in 1943, when it hauled

ERVING 5 IMPORTANT GATEWAYS

★ CHICAGO

★ ST. PAUL--MINNEAPOLIS

★ COUNCIL BLUFFS--OMAHA

★ KANSAS CITY

★ ST. JOSEPH

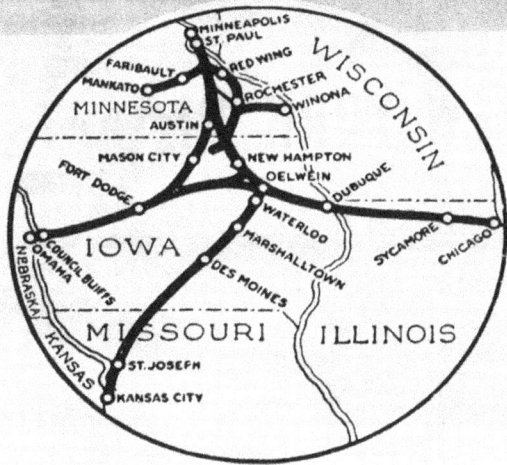

9,286,188 tons. This freight advertisement was published during that year. (Author's collection.)

The diesel-electric locomotive possessed operating features that enabled it to move heavier trains than with steam engines. CGW took advantage of these capabilities by making up massive freight trains with as many as 275 freight cars in one train, thereby reducing the number of freight trains operated. This photograph shows one of these heavy-tonnage trains heading west through Bellwood in 1951. (Author's collection.)

This freight train stretches out of view into the horizon. Movement of such heavy trains placed a tremendous amount of strain on couplers and required expert control of throttle and brake. The photograph was taken at Hayfield, Minnesota, in 1955. (Author's collection.)

Freight Traffic Density

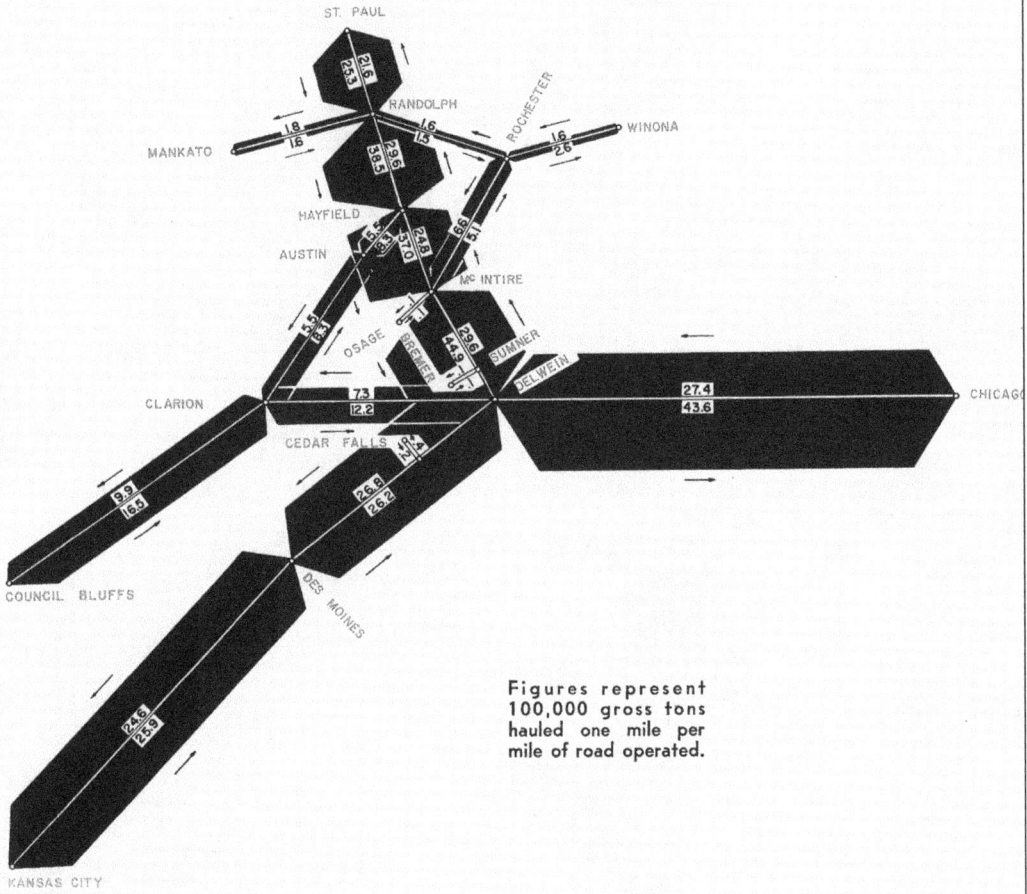

ST. PAUL

RANDOLPH

ROCHESTER

WINONA

MANKATO

HAYFIELD

AUSTIN

Mc INTIRE

SUMNER

OSAGE

BREMER

DELWEIN

CLARION

CHICAGO

CEDAR FALLS

COUNCIL BLUFFS

DES MOINES

KANSAS CITY

21.6
24.3

1.8
1.6

1.6
1.5

1.6
2.6

29.6
38.5

6.6
6.1

24.9
37.0

29.6
14.9

8.1

7.3
12.2

27.4
43.6

26.6
26.2

9.5
16.5

24.6
25.9

Figures represent
100,000 gross tons
hauled one mile per
mile of road operated.

Chicago
GREAT
WESTERN
Railway

CGW published this freight traffic density map in the 1961 annual report. The main line from
and to Chicago usually carried the heaviest amount of traffic, as shown. (Author's collection.)

OPERATING REVENUES

for 1963, as shown on page twenty-four,
are separated as between the various
classes of traffic.

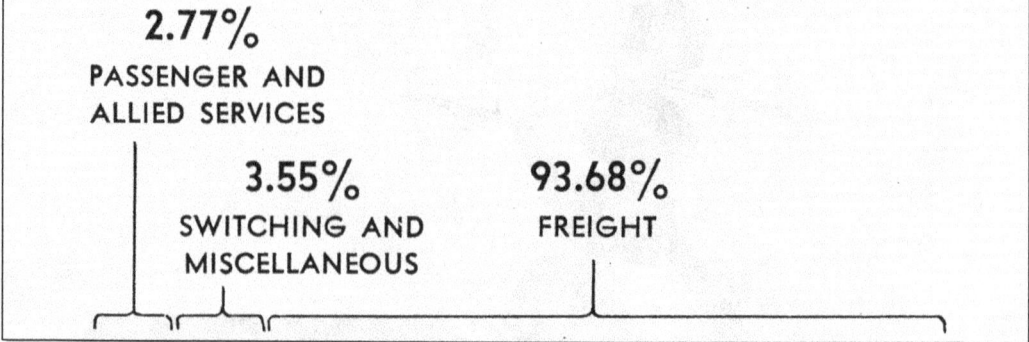

2.77%

PASSENGER AND
ALLIED SERVICES

3.55%   **93.68%**

SWITCHING AND   FREIGHT
MISCELLANEOUS

Freight business always accounted for the largest percentage of annual earnings, as shown in this graph from the 1963 annual report. The small percentage attributed to passenger service was similar for most railroads. In 1960, the railroad industry handled only 27 percent of intercity commercial passenger traffic, with the remainder divided among airlines and bus companies. (Author's collection.)

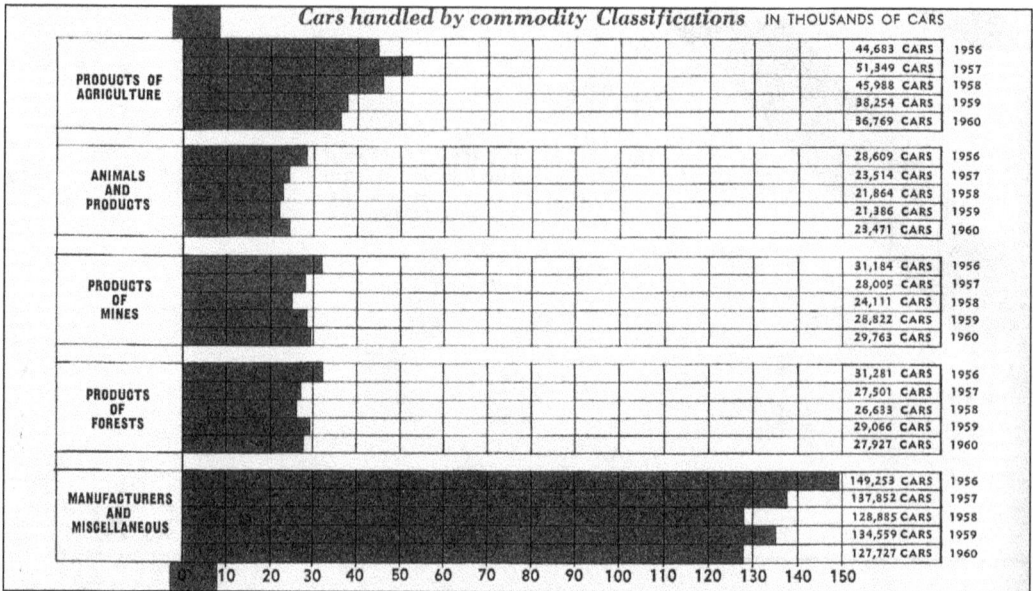

Cars handled by commodity Classifications   IN THOUSANDS OF CARS

Commodity	Cars	Year
PRODUCTS OF AGRICULTURE	44,683 CARS	1956
	51,349 CARS	1957
	45,988 CARS	1958
	38,254 CARS	1959
	36,769 CARS	1960
ANIMALS AND PRODUCTS	28,609 CARS	1956
	23,514 CARS	1957
	21,864 CARS	1958
	21,386 CARS	1959
	23,471 CARS	1960
PRODUCTS OF MINES	31,184 CARS	1956
	28,005 CARS	1957
	24,111 CARS	1958
	28,822 CARS	1959
	29,763 CARS	1960
PRODUCTS OF FORESTS	31,281 CARS	1956
	27,501 CARS	1957
	26,633 CARS	1958
	29,066 CARS	1959
	27,927 CARS	1960
MANUFACTURERS AND MISCELLANEOUS	149,253 CARS	1956
	137,852 CARS	1957
	128,885 CARS	1958
	134,559 CARS	1959
	127,727 CARS	1960

10 20 30 40 50 60 70 80 90 100 110 120 130 140 150

The types of commodities transported by CGW are shown on this graph published in the 1961 annual report. Products of agriculture were always an important source of business because the company served the country's breadbasket. In 1920, CGW established an agricultural development department, which solicited business from farmers and conducted institutes on better farming practices. Eighty-seven institutes were held in 1925, as an example, attended by 17,016 people. (Author's collection.)

48

Graph showing the increasing percentage of our total traffic originating on line compared to percentage received from connecting carriers, which is indicative of our progressive industrial development program.

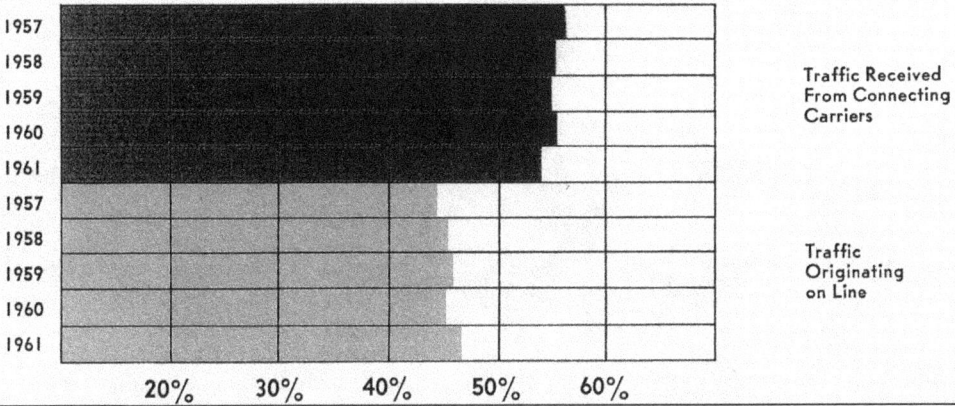

Year						Traffic Received From Connecting Carriers
1957						
1958						
1959						
1960						
1961						
1957						Traffic Originating on Line
1958						
1959						
1960						
1961						
	20%	30%	40%	50%	60%	

Efforts to develop online industries began years before this chart was published in the 1961 annual report. Examples of this activity include the acquisition of a large tract of land west of St. Charles, Illinois, in 1893 for an industrial town and development of a 6,250-acre industrial district at Roseport, Minnesota, in 1954. (Author's collection.)

Locomotive Nos. 108-A and 116-A were photographed pushing freight cars onto a yard track at Chicago Transfer Yard on July 15, 1967. Note the load of steel coils in the gondola car behind the last engine. (Author's collection.)

This photograph shows a freight train passing through Elmhurst, Illinois, in 1966. Four of the company's fleet of eight GP-30 diesels were assigned to this particular train. (Author's collection.)

Westbound manifest train No. 91 was photographed at Ingalton, Illinois, in January 1968. This image clearly shows the benefits of using more powerful locomotives. Only three SD-40 diesels were required to power this freight train instead of four GP-30 engines or six cab units. (Author's collection.)

CGW was one of the first railroads to provide trailer-on-flatcar (TOFC) service when it began transporting semitrailers between Chicago and Minneapolis–St. Paul on July 6, 1936. The company also patented equipment to secure the trailer on the flatcar, as depicted in this patent drawing. Note the use of chains and turnbuckles to attach the trailer to anchor rails on the flatcar deck. (Author's collection.)

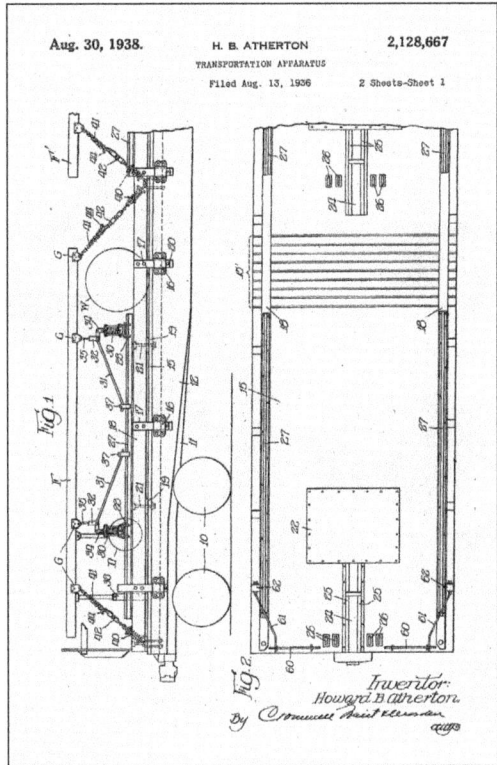

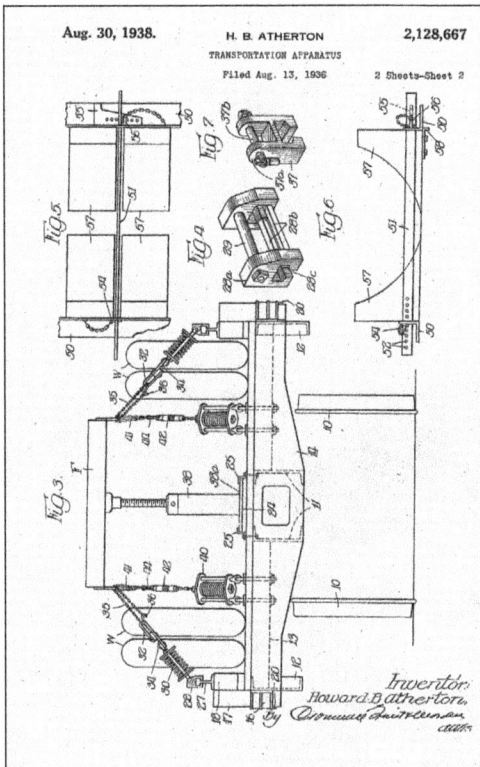

This is the second sheet of the patent drawing, and it shows the use of an adjustable jack to support the front end of the trailer. Other components included wheel chocks and ramps for loading and unloading the trailer. The patent was No. 2,128,667, dated August 30, 1938. (Author's collection.)

CGW transported 10,296 trailers for 20 motortruck companies during the first year of TOFC service from July 1936 to July 1937. The operation was considered a success, with 96 percent on-time delivery, no pilferage, and only minimal damage to freight. This photograph shows the trailer ramp at Chicago Transfer Yard. (Author's collection.)

Piggyback business was actively promoted and expanded starting in 1962. To accommodate shipments, CGW joined the national piggyback pool of Trailer Train in February 1961 to obtain flatcars and leased 100 refrigerated trailers in 1963 for transporting perishables. Also in 1963, trailer ramps were constructed at several stations, which resulted in a total of 16 terminals equipped with ramps to load and unload trailers. (Author's collection.)

Four

PASSENGER SERVICE

This advertisement from 1896 informed patrons that CGW made traveling a luxury. The lady gazing out the window seems relaxed and ready for a peaceful nap. A time card effective May 10, 1896, shows that daily (except Sunday) passenger service at Chicago consisted of six eastbound and seven westbound trains. Only four trains were operated in either direction on Sunday. (Author's collection.)

CGW began an advertising campaign in the summer of 1905, promoting itself as "the Right Road" for traveling from Chicago to Minnesota, Iowa, and other western destinations. The advertisements featured this slogan and a caricature of a Pullman porter who symbolized attentive service. The promotion ceased in 1908, when the company was in receivership. This particular advertisement includes the Pullman porter watching a passenger train, with locomotive No. 904 at the head end, departing Grand Central Station, Chicago. (Author's collection).

Another 1905 advertisement again shows locomotive No. 904 at night with a city landscape illuminated by its headlight. Note the Pullman porter is also present, chatting with the train crew. One can imagine that this advertisement and the one above depicted passenger train No. 3, the daily Twin City Day Express, which departed Chicago at 8:45 a.m. and arrived at Minneapolis at 9:50 p.m. (Author's collection).

CHICAGO—DES MOINES—ROCHESTER—ST. PAUL—
MINNEAPOLIS. NOTE THE AUTOMATIC SAFETY
SIGNAL PROTECTION.

The Great Western Limited, consisting of locomotive No. 509, a tender full of coal, baggage car, and coaches, travels along a substantial ballasted right-of-way protected with fencing and automatic signals. Only a small amount of smoke belches from the smokestack due to skillful firing by an experienced fireman and a locomotive that is properly maintained, sparing passengers from soot and cinders. The Great Western Limited was a daily overnight luxury train that entered service in July 1898 between Chicago and Minneapolis–St. Paul. (James L. Rueber.)

Front and back covers of the December 1, 1906, passenger timetable are shown here. The system map in the maple leaf shows the extent of the company's expansion efforts during the early years of the 20th century. There are now branch lines in Minnesota and Iowa and an extension to Omaha. (Author's collection.)

CHICAGO GREAT WESTERN RAILWAY

CHICAGO ST. PAUL MINNEAPOLIS AND THE NORTHWEST

DEC. 1, 1906.

CHICAGO GREAT WESTERN RAILWAY

COUNCIL BLUFFS OMAHA DES MOINES ST. JOSEPH KANSAS CITY AND THE SOUTHWEST

DEC. 1, 1906.

CHICAGO GREAT WESTERN RY.
"The Maple Leaf Route"
LOCAL TIME TABLES
Chicago to Dubuque, St. Paul and Minneapolis.

Mls. fr. Chic'o	STATIONS	1 LIMITED DAILY	5 EXPRESS DAILY	3 MAIL DAILY	7 DAILY	13 DAILY EX. SUN.
0	Lv CHICAGO	D 6.30 PM	11.30 PM	8.45 AM		7 00 AM
5	Lv FOREST HOME		A 11.55 PM		F 3 25 PM	7 25 AM
7	Lv MAYWOOD		A 11.57 PM		F 3 27 PM	7 28 AM
12	Lv SOUTH ELMHURST		A 12 04 AM		3 38 PM	7 38 AM
16	Lv LOMBARD		A 12 10 AM		3 46 PM	7 46 AM
18	Lv N. GLEN ELLYN		A 12 15 AM		3 50 PM	7 49 AM
21	Lv GRETNA		A 12 18 AM		3 59 PM	7 56 AM
26	Lv INGALTON		A 12 23 AM		4 14 PM	8 04 AM
31	Lv ST. CHARLES		12.33 AM	A 9.41 AM	4 28 PM	8 14 AM
36	Lv WASCO		A 12.41 AM		4 42 PM	8 25 AM
40	Lv LILY LAKE		A 12.49 AM		4 55 PM	8 33 AM
44	Lv VIRGIL		A 12.59 AM		5 05 PM	8 39 AM
46	Lv RICHARDSON		A 12.56 AM		5 14 PM	8 42 AM
59	Lv DE KALB					
52	Lv SYCAMORE	8.00 PM	1.08 AM	10.13 AM	5 28 PM	8 55 AM
59	Lv CLARE		A 1.18 AM		5 43 PM	9 05 AM
65	Lv ESMOND		A 1.27 AM		5 52 PM	9 16 AM
70	Lv LINDENWOOD		F 1.35 AM		6 01 PM	9 24 AM
74	Lv HOLCOMB		F 1.40 AM		6 07 PM	9 30 AM
78	Lv STILLMAN VALLEY		F 1.45 AM		6 17 PM	9 40 AM
83	Lv BYRON	8.50 PM	1.56 AM	A 10.55 AM	6 25 PM	9 50 AM
89	Lv MYRTLE				ARRIVE	F 10 00 AM
91	Lv EGAN					F 10 05 AM
96	Lv GERMAN VALLEY		A 2.14 AM			10 14 AM
102	Lv SOUTH FREEPORT	E 9.17M	2.27 AM	A 11.24 AM		10 28 AM
108	Lv BOLTON					10 43 AM
115	Lv PEARL CITY		F 2.45 AM			10 53 AM
119	Lv KENT		F 2.52 AM			11 02 AM
125	Lv STOCKTON	9.58 PM	3.08 AM	11.59 AM		11 20 AM
133	Lv WOODBINE		A 3.18 AM			11 31 AM
139	Lv ELIZABETH		A 3.28 AM	A 12.19 PM		11 41 AM
141	Lv NORTH HANOVER		A 3.38 AM			11 47 AM
146	Lv RODDEN		A 3.37 AM			F 11 53 AM
153	Lv GALENA JUNCTION		A 3.53 AM			12 11 PM
167	Lv DUBUQUE	11.20 PM	4.25 AM	1.15 PM		12 35 PM
175	Lv DURANGO		F 4.41 AM	F 1.31 PM		ARRIVE
183	Lv GRAF		F 4.55 AM	F 1.45 PM		
187	Lv KIDDER			F 1.51 PM		
191	Lv FARLEY		5.10 AM	F 2.00 PM		
197	Lv DYERSVILLE	E 12 20 AM	5.25 AM	2.13 PM		
205	Lv ALMORAL		F 5.37 AM	F 2.24 PM		
210	Lv ONEIDA		5.47 AM	2.32 PM		
218	Lv MANCHESTER		† 5.15 AM	2.00 PM		
218	Ar MANCHESTER		6.15 AM	3.45 PM		
215	Lv THORPE		F 5.55 AM	F 2.40 PM		
220	Lv DUNDEE		F 6.03 AM	F 2.46 PM		
225	Lv LAMONT		6.18 AM	2.55 PM		
230	Lv AURORA		6.22 AM	3.04 PM		
235	Lv STANLEY		6.30 AM	3.13 PM		
240	Lv OELWEIN	1.45 AM	M 7.25 AM	3.38 PM		
245	Lv WESTGATE		7.37 AM	3.52 PM		
256	Lv SUMNER	2.18 AM	7.50 AM	4.05 PM		
266	Lv FREDERICKSBURG		8.07 AM	4.24 PM		
270	Lv BOYD		F 8.15 AM	F 4.32 PM		
274	Lv NEW HAMPTON	2.46 AM	8.30 AM	4.40 PM		
279	Lv DEVON		F 8.30 AM	4.48 PM		
285	Lv ALTA VISTA		8.41 AM	5.00 PM		
289	Lv ELMA	8.15 AM	8.40 AM	F 5.07 PM		
294	Lv LOWTHER			F 5.10 PM		
299	Lv RICEVILLE	3.88 AM	9.05 AM	5.24 PM		
305	Lv McINTIRE	F 3.45 AM	9.15 AM	5.34 PM		
307	Lv BAILEY			F 5.38 PM		
314	Lv TAOPI		9.30 AM	5.50 PM		
322	Lv ELKTON		F 9.48 AM	F 6.03 PM		
326	Lv SUTTON		9.30 AM	6.08 PM		7 DAILY
328	Lv RENOVA		F 9.54 AM	6.14 PM		
333	Lv SARGEANT		F 10.08 AM	6.23 PM		7 10 AM
339	Lv HAYFIELD	4.55 AM	10.19 AM	6.39 PM		7 20 AM
344	Lv VLASATY					7 28 AM
348	Lv DODGE CENTER	5.11 AM	10.88 AM	6.55 PM		7 38 AM
353	Lv EDEN		10.47 AM	7.04 PM		7 42 AM
358	Lv WEST CONCORD		10.56 AM	7 12 PM		7 48 AM
362	Lv SKYBURG					7 57 PM
367	Lv KENYON	5.46 AM	11.16 AM	7.30 PM		8 11 AM
374	Lv NERSTRAND					8 36 AM
379	Lv DENNISON					8 57 AM
384	Lv STANTON					9 15 AM
388	Lv RANDOLPH	6.21 AM	11.50 AM	8.05 PM		9 35 AM
415	Ar RED WING	10.45 AM				† 10.45 AM
394	Lv HAMPTON, MINN					F 9.40 AM
396	Lv EMPIRE					F 9.57 AM
402	Lv COATES					F 10.07 AM
404	Lv RICH VALLEY					F 10.13 AM
412	Lv INVER GROVE					F 10 26 AM
415	Lv SOUTH ST. PAUL				8.57 PM	F 10 32 AM
420	Ar ST. PAUL	7.20 AM	12.50 PM	9.10 PM	10.45 AM	
430	Ar MINNEAPOLIS	8 00 AM	1.20 PM	9 50 PM	11 20 AM	

A Stops to receive passengers for Dubuque and beyond or discharge passengers from Chicago.
B Stops to discharge passengers from beyond Orblot; and to take passengers for St. Paul and Minneapolis.
D Dining Car attached. E Stops only on signal.
F Flag stop. M Stops for meals. † Except Sunday. Trains Nos. 1, 3 and 5 are solid through trains Chicago to Minneapolis. For equipment see page 7.

CHICAGO GREAT WESTERN RY.
LOCAL TIME TABLES
Minneapolis and St. Paul to Dubuque and Chicago.

Mls. fr. St. P.	STATIONS	2 LIMITED DAILY	4 EXPRESS DAILY	6 CHIC'O SPL DAILY	8 DAILY
	Lv MINNEAPOLIS	8 00 PM	9 10 AM	10 45 PM	4.35 PM
0	Lv ST. PAUL	8 25 PM	9 40 AM	11 20 AM	5.10 PM
1	Lv WEST ST. PAUL				
5	Lv SOUTH ST. PAUL			11 35 PM	F 5.28 PM
8	Lv INVERGROVE			F 11 40 PM	F 5.28 PM
16	Lv RICH VALLEY			F 11 56 PM	F 5.43 PM
18	Lv COATES			F 12 02 AM	F 5.48 PM
22	Lv EMPIRE			F 12 15 AM	F 5.59 PM
26	Lv HAMPTON MINN			12 26 AM	6.08 PM
59	Lv RED WING	† 4.40 PM			
33	Lv RANDOLPH	9 39 PM	10 40 AM	12 40 AM	6.25 PM
38	Lv STANTON		F 10.46 AM	F 12 48 AM	6.86 PM
41	Lv DENNISON		10 55 AM	F 12 58 AM	6.53 PM
46	Lv NERSTRAND		11 05 AM	F 1 09 AM	7.08 PM
53	Lv KENYON	10 14 PM	11 16 AM	1 23 AM	7.30 PM
58	Lv SKYBURG		F 11 25 AM		7.48 PM
62	Lv WEST CONCORD		11 35 AM	1 45 AM	7.55 PM
67	Lv EDEN		11 48 AM		8.07 PM
72	Lv DODGE CENTER	10 45 PM	11 58 AM	2 06 AM	8.18 PM
76	Lv VLASATY		F 11 59 AM		F 8.25 PM
81	Lv HAYFIELD	11 07 PM	12 12 PM	2 30 AM	8.35 PM
87	Lv SARGEANT		F 12 25 PM	2 44 AM	
92	Lv RENOVA		F 12 35 PM		
96	Lv SUTTON		F 12 43 PM		
98	Lv ELKTON		F 12 47 PM		
106	Lv TAOPI		1 00 PM	3 22 AM	
113	Lv BAILEY		F 1 11 PM		
115	Lv McINTIRE	12 01 AM	1 18 PM	3 45 AM	
121	Lv RICEVILLE	E 12 10 AM	1 27 PM	3 59 AM	
126	Lv LOWTHER		F 1 35 PM		
131	Lv ELMA	12 28 AM	1 45 PM	4 24 AM	
135	Lv ALTA VISTA		1 53 PM	F 4 34 AM	
141	Lv DEVON		2 04 PM		
146	Lv NEW HAMPTON	12 54 AM	2 12 PM	5 00 AM	
150	Lv BOYD		F 2 20 PM	F 5 11 AM	
154	Lv FREDERICKSBURG		2 30 PM	5 28 AM	
164	Lv SUMNER	1.25 AM	2 46 PM	5 45 AM	
172	Lv WESTGATE		2 58 PM	6 00 AM	
180	Lv OELWEIN	2.00 AM	3.20 PM	M 7.00 AM	
185	Lv STANLEY		F 3.31 PM	F 7.11 AM	
190	Lv AURORA		F 3.37 PM	F 7.17 AM	
195	Lv LAMONT		F 3.46 PM	7.25 AM	
200	Lv DUNDEE			F 7.32 AM	
205	Lv THORPE			7.38 AM	
210	Lv ONEIDA		4 09 PM	7.48 AM	
218	Lv MANCHESTER		2.00 PM	7 15 AM	
218	Ar MANCHESTER		5.45 PM	8 10 AM	
214	Lv ALMORAL			F 7.54 AM	
223	Lv DYERSVILLE	N 2 50 AM	4.27 PM	8.06 AM	
227	Lv FARLEY			F 8.16 AM	
233	Lv KIDDER			F 8.23 AM	14 DAILY EX. SUN.
237	Lv GRAF			F 8.35 AM	
245	Lv DURANGO			F 8.45 AM	
253	Lv DUBUQUE	4.00 AM	5.25 PM	9.05 AM	2.15 PM
267	Lv GALENA JUNCTION			9.29 AM	2.39 PM
274	Lv RODDEN				F 2.50 PM
279	Lv NORTH HANOVER				3.02 PM
282	Lv ELIZABETH		6.17 PM	9.57 AM	3 10 PM
287	Lv WOODBINE				3 20 PM
294	Lv STOCKTON	5.17 AM	6.42 PM	10.22 AM	3 48 PM
301	Lv KENT				3.58 PM
305	Lv PEARL CITY			H 10.36 AM	4 07 PM
311	Lv BOLTON				4 20 PM
318	Lv SOUTH FREEPORT	N 5.48 AM	H 7.15 PM	10.55 AM	4 30 PM
324	Lv GERMAN VALLEY				4 49 PM
329	Lv EGAN				DAILY 4 57 PM
331	Lv MYRTLE				4 42 PM
337	Lv BYRON	D 6.18 AM	H 7.40 PM	11.20 AM	6.45 AM	5 03 PM
342	Lv STILLMAN VALLEY			F 11.28 AM	6.58 AM	5 03 PM
346	Lv HOLCOMB				7.00 AM	5 18 PM
350	Lv LINDENWOOD				7.05 AM	5 10 PM
355	Lv ESMOND				7.14 AM	5 27 PM
361	Lv CLARE				7.22 AM	5 35 PM
374	Ar DE KALB					
368	Lv SYCAMORE	7.10 AM	8.39 PM	12.15 PM	7.41 AM	5 52 PM
374	Lv RICHARDSON				7.55 AM	5 00 PM
377	Lv VIRGIL				8.03 AM	6 04 PM
380	Lv LILY LAKE				8.13 AM	6 10 PM
384	Lv WASCO				8.25 AM	6 17 PM
389	Lv ST. CHARLES	T 7.40 AM	T 9.05 PM	12.48 PM	8.37 AM	6 27 PM
394	Lv INGALTON				8.48 AM	6 34 PM
399	Lv GRETNA				9.05 AM	6 43 PM
402	Lv N. GLEN ELLYN				9.09 AM	6 47 PM
404	Lv LOMBARD				9.22 AM	6 52 PM
408	Lv SOUTH ELMHURST				9.30 AM	F 7 01 PM
411	Lv BELLEWOOD				F 9.36 AM	
413	Lv MAYWOOD				F 9.38 AM	7 12 PM
415	Ar FOREST HOME				F 9.40 AM	7 15 PM
420	Ar CHICAGO	8.45 AM	10.20 PM	1.40 PM	10.40 AM	7 40 PM

D Dining Car attached. E Stops only on signal. F Flag stop. H Stops to receive passengers for points beyond Orblot at which train stops above. M Stops for meals. N Stops to discharge passengers from Dubuque and beyond or to receive passengers for Chicago. T Stops to discharge passengers from Minneapolis to Chicago. For equipment see page 8. Trains Nos. 2, 4 and 6 are solid through trains Minneapolis to Chicago.

This schedule of passenger trains operating between Chicago and Minneapolis–St. Paul was published in the 1906 timetable. There were five westbound trains and four eastbound. Railroads use odd numbers to designate trains headed west and even numbers east. (Author's collection.)

56

Shown here are the front and back covers of the September 3, 1921, passenger timetable. CGW replaced the maple leaf trademark in June 1910 with a circular emblem containing ears of corn and a new slogan: the Corn Belt Route. CGW chose the new trademark because it served the Corn Belt, an agricultural region in the Midwest where corn acreage once exceeded that of any other crop. (Author's collection.)

CHICAGO
GREAT WESTERN

CHICAGO
GREAT WESTERN

CORN BELT ROUTE

CORN BELT ROUTE

COUNCIL BLUFFS - OMAHA
DES MOINES - ST. JOSEPH
KANSAS CITY
AND THE
SOUTHWEST

CHICAGO
ST. PAUL
MINNEAPOLIS
AND THE
NORTHWEST

Corrected to September 3, 1921

Corrected to September 3, 1921

It Has
No
Peer

THE
GREAT WESTERN LIMITED
Between
CHICAGO AND ST. PAUL - MINNEAPOLIS
Lv. Chicago - - 6.30 P.M.
Ar. St. Paul - 7.30 A.M.
Ar. Minneapolis 8.10 A.M.
THRU ROCHESTER SLEEPER ON THIS TRAIN
AN ALL-STEEL TRAIN WITH CHUMMY CLUB CAR AND DINER
For fares and sleeping car reservations call upon any
agent, representative or write
W. R. MacFARLAND, General Passenger Agent, C. G. W. R. R.,
1139 Peoples Gas Bldg., Chicago, Ill.

Advertisements on passenger service during the 1920s and 1930s displayed a different emblem without the Corn Belt Route slogan. The design featured the company name with Great Western emphasized in uppercase letters inside a circle with a steam locomotive depicted as traveling at high speed. The new logo was prominently displayed in this 1921 advertisement. (Author's collection.)

Chicago, Dubuque—Rochester, St. Paul, Minneapolis

For complete local schedules between Oelwein and St. Paul see Tables 1 and 5

Read Down   **Read Up**

31 DAILY	3 DAILY	5 DAILY	1 DAILY	Mls	TABLE 6	2 DAILY	6 DAILY	4 DAILY	32 DAILY
PM	AM	PM	PM			AM	AM	PM	AM
2 45	7 30	11 00	G6 30	0	Lv....Chicago....Ar	G8 40	7 30	7 55	11 00
3 15	7 55	11 25	R6 55	10	Lv...Forest Park...Lv	R8 13	m & i	7 17	9 55
3 20	7 58	..a..	b..	12	Lv....Maywood....Lv	g..	m & o	..h..	9 51
f 3 23	f 8 01			13	Lv...Bellewood...Lv	g..	..m...		f 9 47
f 3 30	f 8 07	..a..	b..	17	Lv...Elmhurst....Lv	g..	m & o	..h..	f 9 41
3 38	f 8 13			21	Lv....Lombard....Lv	g..	m & o		9 34
3 43	f 8 16			23	Lv.North Glen EllynLv	g..	..m...		9 27
3 53	f 8 20			26	Lv....Gretna....Lv	g..	..m...		9 20
4 10	f 8 30			31	Lv....Ingalton....Lv	g..	..m...		9 00
4 24	8 42	12 05	7 35	36	Lv...St. Charles...Lv	7 37	..m...	6 32	8 42
f 4 26	f...			37	Lv....Fox River....Lv	g..	c m..		f 8 36
4 40	8 52	a & d		41	Lv.....Wasco.....Lv	g..	..m...	f 6 20	8 31
4 51	9 01	a & d		46	Lv....Lily Lake....Lv	g..	..m...	f 6 13	8 19
4 58	f 9 06	a & d		49	Lv.....Virgil.....Lv	g..	..m...	f 6 08	8 08
5 10	9 11	a & d		51	Lv...Richardson....Lv	g..	..m...	f 6 03	7 57
5 25	9 24	12 43	8 14	57	Lv...Sycamore....Lv	7 05	5 54	5 51	7 36
Electric	line bet	ween Sy	camore	and	....DeKalb......	DeKalb	See page 39		
5 37	f 9 33		b..	62	Lv....Wilkinson...Lv	g..	..m...		7 22
5 43	9 37	a..	b..	64	Lv.....Clare.....Lv	g..	..m...	f 5 32	7 18
5 54	9 45	a..	b..	70	Lv....Esmond....Lv	g..	..m...	f 5 22	7 09
6 05	9 53	a..	b..	75	Lv..Lindenwood...Lv	g..	..m...	f 5 13	7 01
6 12	9 59	a..	b..	78	Lv....Holcomb....Lv	g..	..m...	5 05	6 56
6 20	10 08	a..	b..	83	Lv.Stillman Valley.Lv	g..	..m...	4 54	6 48
6 28	10 17	1 35	9 04	88	Lv.....Byron.....Lv	6 17	..m...	4 45	6 40
PM	10 29		b..	94	Lv.....Myrtle.....Lv	g..	..m...	f 4 29	AM
	10 36	a..	b..	97	Lv......Egan......Lv	g..	..m...	f 4 19	
	10 46	a..	b..	101	Lv.....Meekin.....Lv	g..	..m...	4 10	
	10 58	2 06	9 37	107	Lv..So. Freeport..Lv	f 5 47	m & o	3 58	
..gg..	..gg..	..gg..			......Freeport......	..gg..	..gg..	..gg..	
	11 10		b..	114	Lv.....Bolton.....Lv	g..	..m...	f 3 43	
	11 25	f 2 27	f 9 58	120	Lv...Pearl City...Lv	g..	..m...	3 32	
	11 38	a..	b..	125	Lv......Kent......Lv	g..	..m...	f 3 19	
	11 56	2 55	10 25	131	Lv....Stockton...Lv	5 03	..m...	3 00	
	12 08	a..	b..	139	Lv...Woodbine...Lv	g..	..m...	2 47	
	12 18	3 17	10 45	143	Lv...Elizabeth...Lv	f 4 40	..m...	2 36	
	12 27	a..	b..	147	Lv.North Hanover..Lv	g..	..m...	2 25	
	† 1 00				Ar.....Hanover.....Lv			† 1 40	
	12 33		b..	150	Lv.....Rodden.....Lv	g..	..m...	f 2 17	
	f 12 39		b..	152	Lv....Winston....Lv	g..	..m...		
	f 12 43		b..	154	Lv......Rice......Lv	g..	..m...		
	f 12 46		b..	155	Lv.....Aiken.....Lv	g..	..m...	f 2 04	
	12 50	f 3 41	f 11 11	158	Lv..Galena Junct..Lv	g..	..m...	1 59	
	1 13	4 05	11 35	172	Ar....Dubuque...Lv	3 50	2 52	1 34	
	1 19	4 13	11 40	172	Lv....Dubuque...Ar	3 45	2 47	1 27	
	1 37	h & k	b..	180	Lv....Durango...Lv	g..	..m...	f 1 08	
	f 1 42		b..	183	Lv......Budd......Lv	g..	..m...	f 1 02	
	1 52	h & k	b..	188	Lv......Graf......Lv	g..	..m...	f 12 52	
	f 2 00		b..	192	Lv.....Kidder.....Lv	g..	..m...	f 12 41	
	2 13	h & k	b..	196	Lv.....Farley.....Lv	g..	..m...	f 12 33	
	2 23	5 16	f 12 38	203	Lv...Dyersville...Lv	j..	m & e	12 23	
	f 2 31	h & k	b..	208	Lv..Petersburg...Lv	g..	..m..	f 12 13	
	2 35		b..	211	Lv....Almoral....Lv	g..	..m..	f 12 08	
	2 42	5 38	b..	215	Lv.....Oneida.....Lv	g..	..m..	12 01	
	† 3 10			223	Ar...Manchester...Lv			†11 30	
				223	Lv...Manchester...Ar				
	2 50	h & k	b..	220	Lv.....Thorpe.....Lv	g..	..m..	f 11 50	
	2 58	h & k	b..	225	Lv....Dundee....Lv	g..	..m..	11 41	
	3 06	6 03	b c d q	230	Lv....Lamont....Lv	g..	m o e v	11 31	
	3 17	6 12	b..	235	Lv.....Aurora.....Lv	g..	..m..	11 22	
	3 27	6 21	b..	240	Lv.....Stanley.....Lv	g..	..m..	11 12	
	3 40	6 35	1 45	246	Ar..Oelwein l, 9..Lv	1 45	12 50	11 00	
	PM	6 55	2 00	246	Lv.....Oelwein.....Ar	1 30	AM	AM	
		7 09		254	Lv...Westgate l...Lv				
		7 22	2 24	261	Lv...Sumner l, 4..Lv	12 56			
		7 40		271	Lv Fredericksburg l Lv				
		f 7 50		276	Lv.....Boyd l.....Lv				
		7 58	2 52	280	Lv New Hampton l Lv	12 28			
		f 8 06		285	Lv....Devon l....Lv				
		8 15		291	Lv...Alta Vista l..Lv				
		8 22	3 16	294	Lv.....Elma l.....Lv	f 12 07			
		f 8 32		300	Lv.....Acme l.....Lv				
		8 42		305	Lv...Riceville l...Lv	f 11 50			
		8 53	3 42	310	Ar..McIntire l, 5..Lv	11 35			
		†11 05	6 30	359	Ar....Rochester...Lv	9 20			
		9 54	4 33	344	Ar...Hayfield l, 7..Lv	10 37			
		10 15	5 00	353	Ar..Dodge Center..Lv	10 17			
		10 48	5 44	372	Ar....Kenyon l, 2..Lv	9 46			
		11 47	6 15	392	Ar Randolph l, 2, 5 Lv	9 11			
		12 45	f & n	420	Ar...So. St. Paul...Lv	..l..			
		1 00	7 30	425	Ar.....St. Paul.....Lv	8 10			
		1 40	8 10	435	Ar..Minneapolis...Lv	7 40			
		PM	AM			PM			

ON YOUR NEXT TRIP BETWEEN

Chicago AND **St. Paul-Minneapolis**

USE THE "Great Western Limited"

Fast and comfortable— You'll feel like at home

The passenger schedule from the 1921 timetable shows four trains in each direction between Chicago and Minneapolis–St. Paul. CGW began to experience a decline in passenger business starting in 1920 due to the use of automobiles. The company was especially susceptible to loss of business to the automobile because the distance between terminals was short enough to be easily traveled by car in a day or two. (Author's collection.)

CGW responded to the decline in passenger business by offering travelers convenient and fast schedules, special amenities aboard trains, and modernized equipment. This advertisement from 1921 proclaimed transit time between Minneapolis–St. Paul was shortened by two hours due to eliminating 27 stops. (Author's collection.)

THE

STRONG LINE
BETWEEN
Kansas City and St. Paul - Minneapolis

All steel trains over a time tested well ballasted roadbed insures comfort and safety.

NORTHBOUND				SOUTHBOUND			
	Great Western Limited	Great Western Express	Iowa Express		Kansas City Limited	Southwestern Limited	Waterloo-Des Moines Express
Lv KANSAS CITY....	2.30 p.m.	11.30 p.m.	9.00 a.m.	Lv MINNEAPOLIS	1.55 p.m.	7.40 p.m.	8.25 a.m.
Ar DES MOINES....	9.30 p.m.	7.15 a.m.	5.15 p.m.	Lv ST.PAUL	2.30 p.m.	8.10 p.m.	9.00 a.m.
Ar ST.PAUL.	7.30 a.m.	3.59 p.m.	....	Ar DES MOINES....	11.15 p.m.	*5.50 a.m.	8.35 p.m.
Ar MINNEAPOLIS ..	8.10 a.m.	4.40 p.m.	....	Ar KANSAS CITY	7.45 a.m.	12.55 p.m.	....

* Berger may be accepted until 7.30 A.M.

27 stops cut out—over 2 hours faster time.

Between Kansas City and Des Moines the Chicago Great Western Railroad operates more trains daily than any other line—it is the short line and makes the fastest time.

for economy, safety, comfort and speed—rain or shine—

Travel
by Great Western

$18.00
Round Trip
between

Chicago - St. Paul - Minneapolis

In Effect Daily
15-Day Limit

Tickets Good in Free Reclining
Chair Cars and Coaches on

the Legionnaire

6:30 pm Lv. .. Chicago .. Ar. 8:18 am
7:10 am Ar. .. St. Paul .. Lv. 8:20 pm
7:50 am Ar. .. Minneapolis .. Lv. 7:45 pm
Tickets and full information from
Great Western Agents or

E. W. IRELAND, General Passenger Agent
122 S. Michigan Blvd., Chicago, Ill.

Chicago Great Western

CGW held a nationwide contest in 1924 to rename the Great Western Limited, and it selected the Legionnaire, submitted by four people (each received a prize of $50). The name was chosen to honor the men who served in the armed forces during World War I. The Legionnaire was officially inaugurated on January 16, 1925. CGW publicized the luxury train with phrases such as "You'll find luxurious comfort and warm-blooded hospitality built right into this popular train." This advertisement was published in 1929. (Author's collection.)

59

The most comfortable way

to **Rochester**

MINNESOTA

FINE TRAINS, SMOOTH TRACK,
AUTOMATIC SAFETY SIGNALS
and ON-TIME ARRIVALS

Great Western with its rails connecting Rochester and Chicago, Minneapolis, St. Paul, Omaha and Kansas City is the connecting link between this important city and the rest of the continent and offers train service that is satisfyingly good in every particular; Pullmans of the latest type, observation and club cars—and wonderful meals at very moderate prices.

REDUCED FARES

Reduced fare tickets are on sale every day from your home town to Rochester via Great Western—six months return limit. Be sure to specify GREAT WESTERN from Chicago, Omaha, Kansas City or Twin Cities to Rochester.

GREAT WESTERN STATIONS
CONVENIENTLY LOCATED

The Chicago Great Western Station in Rochester is conveniently located in the heart of the downtown district, close to the leading hotels.

Great Western trains enter and depart from Burlington Station at Omaha, and Union Stations at Kansas City and the Twin Cities.

In Chicago, Grand Central Station is only two blocks from the Loop—no bridges to cross—no stairs to climb.

WRITE FOR THIS BOOKLET

Descriptive booklet "The Way to Rochester, Minn.," giving complete train service, hotel rates and information of interest to the Rochester traveler, sent free on request to

E. W. Ireland, General Passenger Agent
122 South Michigan Blvd., Chicago, Ill.

Chicago Great Western

Rochester, Minnesota, was an important source of passenger business partly due to the world-famous Mayo Clinic. CGW attracted travelers to Rochester by offering trains that provided various amenities for their comfort and dining service that featured "a hint of Old Virginia in the cooking." Famous CGW passenger trains that served Rochester included the *Red Bird* and the *Blue Bird*, which provided service from and to Minneapolis–St. Paul. (Author's collection.)

CGW also offered service outside of its territory through connections with other railroads and a combined rail and air service. This 1929 advertisement provided information and a schedule for sleeping car service from Minneapolis–St. Paul to Los Angeles through connections with the Atchison, Topeka and Santa Fe Railroad. (Author's collection.)

to **Santa Fe** through sleeping cars
the Grand Canyon way

California

First—straight south to warmer weather—then westward under southern skies through the colorful, romantic Navajo country of New Mexico and Arizona to Pasadena and Los Angeles. Service begins October 15.

SCHEDULE

Standard Pullmans Grand Canyon Limited*	*Note—Cars run on following dates from Minneapolis-St. Paul
Lv. Minneapolis . . . 3:30 pm	October 15, 17, 19, 22, 24, 26, 29, 31.
Lv. St. Paul . . . . . 4:00 pm	November 2, 5, 7, 9, 12, 14, 16, 19, 21, 23, 26, 28, 30.
Lv. Kansas City . . 10:00 am	December—Every day except December 22, 23, 24, 25.
Ar. Pasadena. . . . . 1:45 pm	January—Every day.
Ar. Los Angeles . . . 2:15 pm	February—Every day to and including February 28, 1930.

Get booklets, full information and reservations from

Minneapolis Ticket Office
522 Second Ave. South
Phone Main 3561

St. Paul Ticket Office
4th and Robert Sts.
Phone Riverview 4200

C. J. BROOKS, District Passenger Agent
522 Second Ave. South, Minneapolis

· Great Western-Santa Fe ·

Shown here are the front and back covers of the May 1, 1936, passenger timetable. CGW revised the Corn Belt Route trademark during the 1930s to present a modern, austere appearance. (Author's collection.)

CHICAGO GREAT WESTERN · CORN BELT ROUTE · WESTERN RAILROAD CO.

TIME TABLES

•

Minneapolis
St. Paul-Omaha
Des Moines
St. Joseph
Kansas City
and the
Southwest

•

**CHICAGO
GREAT WESTERN**

CHICAGO GREAT WESTERN · CORN BELT ROUTE · WESTERN RAILROAD CO.

TIME TABLES

•

Chicago
Dubuque
Rochester
St. Paul
Minneapolis
and the
Northwest

•

**CHICAGO
GREAT WESTERN**

⅓ SAVING

ON OVERNIGHT TRAVEL BETWEEN

CHICAGO

AND

St. Paul - Minneapolis

THE CHICAGO GREAT WESTERN announces new lows for travel between Chicago and the Twin Cities. New type nicely upholstered tourist sleeping cars — comfortable berths — popular priced meals. Early morning arrival assures a full business day.

FARES

BETWEEN CHICAGO AND	ONE WAY	ROUND TRIP
St. Paul	$7.93	$14.28
Minneapolis	8.15	14.67

Comfortable Berths Assure a Good Night's Rest
Lower Berth $1.25

Two persons in berth for price of one, if desired. Children — half fare. Round trip fares at similar reductions.

Although CGW was in receivership when this advertisement was published in 1936, the company reduced fares between Chicago and Minneapolis–St. Paul in an effort to increase business. (Author's collection.)

Chicago, Dubuque— Rochester, St. Paul, Minneapolis

(For complete local schedules Oelwein and St. Paul, see Tables 1 and 3)

Read Down				Read Up	
3 DAILY EX. SAT (MOTOR)	**1-21** DAILY	MLS.	**TABLE 2**	**26-2** DAILY	**4** DAILY EX. SUN. MOTOR
PM	PM		*Central Time*	AM	PM
†11 30	7 30	0	Lv....Chicago....Ar	8 30	† 7 30
11 55	7 52	10	Lv....Forest Park.....Lv	8 08	6 55
.....	..q..	12	Lv....Maywood.....Lv	..m..	f 6 50
.....	..q..	13	Lv....Bellewood.....Lv	..m..	.....
12 07	..q..	17	Lv....Elmhurst.....Lv	..m..	6 38
f12 11	..q..	19	Lv....Villa Park.....Lv	..m..	f 6 33
f12 16	..q..	21	Lv....Lombard.....Lv	..m..	.....
f12 25	..q..	26	Lv....Gretna.....Lv	..m..	f 6 20
f12 33	..q..	31	Lv....Ingalton....Lv	..m..	.....
12 45	8 28	36	Lv....St. Charles.....Lv	7 32	6 01
.....	..q..	37	Lv....Fox River.....Lv	..m..	.....
f12 56	..q..	41	Lv....Wasco.....Lv	..m..	f 5 44
f 1 06	..q..	46	Lv....Lily Lake.....Lv	..m..	f 5 37
f 1 10	..q..	49	Lv....Virgil.....Lv	..m..	f 5 30
f 1 14	..q..	51	Lv....Richardson.....Lv	..m..	f 5 20
1 31	8 58	57	Lv....Sycamore.....Lv	7 01	5 11
..c..	..c..	...	Lv....DeKalb.....Lv	..c..	..c..
f 1 41	..q..	62	Lv....Wilkinson.....Lv	..m..	.....
1 48	..q..	64	Lv....Clare.....Lv	..m..	f 4 55
1 59	..q..	70	Lv....Esmond.....Lv	..m..	f 4 44
f 2 09	..q..	75	Lv....Lindenwood....Lv	..m..	f 4 35
f 2 16	f 9 27	78	Lv....Holcomb.....Lv	..m..	4 29
f 2 25	..q..	83	Lv....Stillman Valley...Lv	..m..	4 20
2 35	9 41	88	Lv....Byron.....Lv	6 17	4 12
f 2 45	..q..	94	Lv....Myrtle.....Lv	..m..	f 4 03
f 2 52	..q..	97	Lv....Egan.....Lv	..m..	3 57
f 3 02	..q..	101	Lv....German Valley..Lv	..m..	3 49
f 3 12	f10 04	107	Lv....So. Freeport....Lv	f 5 51	3 40
..n..	..n..	...	Lv....Freeport.....Lv	..n..	..n..
f 3 25	..q..	114	Lv....Bolton.....Lv	..m..	f 3 28
f 3 35	f10 21	120	Lv....Pearl City.....Lv	f 5 36	3 20
f 3 45	..q..	125	Lv....Kent.....Lv	..m..	3 11
4 00	10 43	131	Lv....Stockton.....Lv	5 20	3 00
f 4 16	..q..	139	Lv....Woodbine.....Lv	..m..	2 47
4 26	f11 00	143	Lv....Elizabeth.....Lv	f 4 52	2 38
4 34	..q..	147	Lv....North Hanover...Lv	..m..	2 30
f 4 40	..q..	150	Lv....Rodden.....Lv	..m..	2 25
f 4 48	..q..	152	Lv....Winston.....Lv	..m..	.....
f 4 53	..q..	154	Lv....Rice.....Lv	..m..	.....
f 4 56	..q..	155	Lv....Aiken.....Lv	..m..	f 2 12
f 5 02	..q..	158	Lv...Galena Junction..Lv	..m..	2 08
5 35	11 48	172	Ar....Dubuque.....Lv	4 05	1 45
5 35	11 48	172	Lv....Dubuque.....Ar	4 05	1 45
f 5 55	..q..	180	Lv....Durango.....Lv	..m..	f 1 24
f 6 01	..q..	183	Lv....Budd.....Lv	..m..	f 1 19
f 6 12	..q..	188	Lv....Graf.....Lv	..m..	f 1 10
f 6 21	..q..	192	Lv....Kidder.....Lv	..m..	f 1 03
f 6 34	..q..	196	Lv....Farley.....Lv	..m..	f12 55
6 47	f12 52	203	Lv....Dyersville.....Lv	f 3 06	12 44
f 6 57	..q..	208	Lv....Petersburg.....Lv	..m..	f12 36
f 7 04	..q..	211	Lv....Almoral.....Lv	..m..	f12 30
7 15	f 1 10	215	Lv....Oneida.....Lv	..m..	12 23
† 9 00	.....	223	Ar....Manchester.....Lv	.....	†11 55
.....	.....	223	Lv....Manchester.....Ar	.....	†12 50
f 7 27	..q..	220	Lv....Thorpe.....Lv	..m..	f12 15
f 7 38	..q..	225	Lv....Dundee.....Lv	..m..	12 07
7 50	f 1 34	230	Lv....Lamont.....Lv	..m..	11 59
8 00	..q..	235	Lv....Aurora.....Lv	..m..	11 50
8 10	..q..	240	Lv....Stanley.....Lv	..m..	11 41
8 30	2 00	246	Ar....Oelwein 1, 6....Lv	2 05	†11 30
AM	2 15	246	Lv....Oelwein.....Ar	2 00	AM
.....	..s..	254	Lv....Westgate.....Lv	f 1 46	
.....	2 46	261	Lv....Sumner 8.....Lv	1 35	
.....	..s..	271	Lv....Fredericksburg...Lv	f 1 19	
.....	3 20	280	Lv....New Hampton....Lv	1 05	
.....	..s..	291	Lv....Alta Vista.....Lv	f12 49	
.....	..s..	294	Lv....Elma.....Lv	12 44	
.....	..s..	305	Lv....Riceville.....Lv	f12 28	
.....	4 08	310	Ar....McIntire 1, 3....Lv	12 20	
# 7 00	359	Ar....Rochester 3....Lv	*10 00	
.....	5 10	344	Lv....Hayfield 1, 4....Lv	11 20	.....
.....	5 28	353	Lv....Dodge Center....Lv	10 52	.....
.....	a-s..	362	Lv....West Concord....Lv	l-r..	.....
.....	5 58	372	Lv....Kenyon.....Lv	10 22	.....
.....	..s..	378	Lv....Nerstrand.....Lv	..r..	.....
.....	..s..	384	Lv....Dennison.....Lv	..r..	.....
.....	kk-s..	392	Lv....Randolph 1, 3, 7...Lv	9 50	.....
.....	..s..	420	Lv....South St. Paul....Lv	9 05	.....
.....	7 30	425	Ar....St. Paul.....Lv	8 55	.....
.....	8 10	435	Ar....Minneapolis....Lv	8 20	.....
	AM			PM	

Vertical markings: THE MINNESOTAN (under columns 1-21 and 26-2); Runs to Clarion see table 6 (left side, lower); From Kansas City; see tables 1 and 5 (right side, lower).

This schedule for passenger trains between Chicago and Minneapolis–St. Paul was published in the 1936 timetable. The number of trains has been significantly reduced to two each way. Six years previously, in March 1930, the Legionnaire was renamed the Minnesotan. Note that local trains Nos. 3 and 4 were assigned motorcars, which were the mail-express-passenger coaches powered by gasoline engines. (Author's collection.)

CGW published this eye-catching advertisement to promote patronage between Chicago and Des Moines, Iowa. The train was named the Chicago Special, and it featured a dining car, coaches, and sleeping cars. (Author's collection.)

—TO—
Chicago

DES MOINES' OWN TRAIN
Great Western Number Six

Great Western Number Six is a Des Moines train — made up in Des Moines nightly of clean and inviting cars. Leaves Union Station at 9.00 P. M. daily for Chicago. Only five scheduled stops en route. Arrives Chicago — downtown — at 7.30 next morning. Leaves on time — arrives on time.

Equally Attractive Service Westbound

For tickets or reservations, apply or telephone

Consolidated Ticket Office
403 West Walnut Street
Phone Walnut 3270

Union Station
Cherry St., between 5th & 6th
Phone Walnut 447

H. E. REDLINGSHAFER, C. P. A.
W. L. SEELEY; G. A. P. D.
514 Hubbell Building   Phone Market 1134

Des Moines, Iowa

The Minnesotan is eastbound at Sycamore, Illinois. (Joiner History Room, Sycamore, Illinois.)

Motorcar No. M-1006, with baggage car and coach, passes through Elizabeth, Illinois. The train is one of the daily locals that ran between Chicago and Oelwein. (Joiner History Room, Sycamore, Illinois.)

The engineer of steam locomotive No. 756 inspects the valve gear during a stop at Sycamore, Illinois. Note the water hydrant positioned over the tender to refill the tank. The two white flags displayed on the locomotive indicate that it was an extra passenger train not operating by timetable schedule. Although headed east, the extra was on the westbound track to clear the train approaching from the rear. (Joiner History Room, Sycamore, Illinois.)

During World War II, CGW experienced a substantial increase in passenger business, which quickly declined again after the war ended. During the first nine months of 1948, the company sustained a loss of $750,575 from its passenger services. It began an intensive effort to discontinue passenger trains, and more than half of passenger train miles, along with all parlor, buffet, and sleeping car service, were eliminated by 1953. This photograph of the Minnesotan arriving at Chicago in 1949 equipped with a single coach clearly shows the train was lightly patronized by this time. The Minnesotan was discontinued on May 10, 1949. (Joiner History Room, Sycamore, Illinois.)

Chicago
GREAT
WESTERN
Railway

TIME TABLES

Chicago
Kansas City
Minneapolis
St. Paul
St. Joseph
Des Moines
Omaha
Dubuque

EFFECTIVE APRIL 27, 1952

No. 152

Printed in U.S.A.

Chicago
GREAT
WESTERN
Railway

TIME TABLES

Chicago
Kansas City
Minneapolis
St. Paul
St. Joseph
Des Moines
Omaha
Dubuque

EFFECTIVE APRIL 27, 1952

NO. 152

Printed in U.S.A.

Shown here are the front and back covers of the April 27, 1952, passenger timetable. CGW replaced the Corn Belt Route trademark in 1950 with the logo shown. It has been referred to as the "Lucky Strike" emblem after a similar circular trademark used by a popular brand of cigarettes. (Author's collection.)

Local Schedules

Chicago, Dubuque,

Oelwein

Read Down   **Read Up**

7 Daily	Mls	TABLE 3		8 Daily
PM		Central Time (Grand Central Station)		AM
4 30	0	Lv..........Chicago.........Ar		11 00
4 55	10	Lv.........Forest Park	Lv	10 30
4 58	12	Lv.........Maywood........	Lv	10 27
.....	13	Lv.........Bellwood.........	Lv	.....
5 07	17	Lv..........Elmhurst..........	Lv	f10 17
.....	19	Lv.........Villa Park........	Lv	.....
.....	21	Lv.........Lombard.........	Lv	.....
f 5 24	26	Lv..........Gretna..........	Lv	f 9 58
f 5 32	31	Lv..........Ingalton........	Lv	f 9 49
5 43	36	Lv.........St. Charles........	Lv	9 40
5 52	41	Lv...........Wasco.........	Lv	9 27
6 00	46	Lv........Lily Lake........	Lv	9 19
6 05	49	Lv.........Virgil........	Lv	9 13
6 24	57	Lv.........Sycamore.........	Lv	9 00
		..........De Kalb..........		
6 36	64	Lv..........Clare........	Lv	8 39
6 46	70	Lv..........Esmond.........	Lv	8 28
6 55	75	Lv........Lindenwood........	Lv	8 17
7 02	78	Lv.........Holcomb........	Lv	8 10
.....	83	Lv.....Stillman Valley......	Lv	.....
7 22	88	Lv..........Byron..........	Lv	7 50
f 7 32	94	Lv.........Myrtle.........	Lv	f 7 39
.....	97	Lv.........Egan.......	Lv	.....
7 44	101	Lv......German Valley......	Lv	7 25
f 7 52	107	Lv........So. Freeport........	Lv	f 7 15
.....	114	Lv.........Bolton.....	Lv	.....
8 11	120	Lv.........Pearl City........	Lv	6 55
.....	125	Lv...........Kent.........	Lv	.....
8 34	131	Lv.........Stockton.......	Lv	6 35
.....	139	Lv.........Woodbine........	Lv	.....
8 55	143	Lv.........Elizabeth........	Lv	6 00
9 02	147	Lv......North Hanover.......	Lv	5 50
.....	154	Lv...........Rice........	Lv	.....
f 9 18	155	Lv...........Aiken......	Lv	f 5.30
f 9 23	158	Lv......Galena Junction	Lv	5 25
9 51	172	Lv.........Dubuque.......	Lv	5 05
f 9 59	174	Lv........Fair Ground.......	Lv	4 50
.....	180	Lv.........Durango........	Lv	.....
10 25	188	Lv...........Graf........	Lv	4 23
f10 41	196	Lv..........Farley........	Lv	f 4 07
10 55	203	Lv.........Dyersville........	Lv	3 55
11 05	208	Lv.........Petersburg........	Lv	3 42
f11 10	211	Lv..........Almoral.........	Lv	f 3 37
11 19	215	Lv..........Oneida........	Lv	3 30
.....	220	Lv..........Thorpe.........	Lv	.....
.....	225	Lv..........Dundee.........	Lv	.....
11 46	230	Lv.........Lamont........	Lv	2 59
11 55	235	Lv.........Aurora.........	Lv	2 50
.....	240	Lv.........Stanley........	Lv	.....
12 15	246	Ar.........Oelwein 1, 2.	Lv	2 30

The 1952 timetable for Chicago listed only two local trains between Chicago and Oelwein. The number of passenger trains between Chicago and Oelwein was reduced from four to two in 1949 after ridership dropped to an average of 14 passengers per trip westbound and less than eight eastbound. The last two trains were kept in service for carrying U.S. mail. (Author's collection.)

66

A severe blow to the final passenger trains between Chicago and Oelwein occurred in 1953, when CGW lost its mail contract. This postal cover was issued to commemorate the last run of the railway post office (RPO) car that year. (Author's collection.)

This gloomy photograph shows the last run of the RPO car in October 1953. (Joiner History Room, Sycamore, Illinois.)

AUGUST 28, 1956

AN AGE ENDS—Sycamore's last east bound passenger train goes
past the Sycamore depot on the Great Western Railroad. Its final
run was Saturday, August 11, with the last westbound train going
through at 2:25 p.m. Sunday, August 12.

By action of the Interstate Commerce Commission the Great
Western was granted permission to discontinue its last two passenger trains, thereby leaving Sycamore without such service for
the first time since the middle of the last century.

During the last week of its runs through here many citizens
came out for a final look, some taking pictures.

CGW continued to operate the locals between Chicago and Oelwein after the loss of the mail contract. However, during a six-month period from 1955 to 1956, the trains averaged two riders per trip. The loss from providing this service during 1955 totaled $170,000. CGW filed a petition with the ICC in 1956 to end passenger service between Chicago and Oelwein, and the company quickly received approval. This old clipping from a Sycamore newspaper reported on the last runs in August 1956. (Joiner History Room, Sycamore, Illinois.)

By 1965, CGW was operating passenger trains only between Minneapolis–St. Paul and Omaha. Decreasing revenues and increasing expenses forced the company to end this service in September 1965. *Safety News* featured a brief article on this historic event when CGW became a "freight only" railroad. (Author's collection.)

Chicago
GREAT WESTERN Railway

SAFETY NEWS

SEPTEMBER and OCTOBER 1965

Vol. 11   Issued by the Chicago Great Western Railway Co.   V. Allan Vaughn, Edit
Nos. 9 and 10   Oelwein, Iowa   G. L. Vargason, Ass't Edit

End Of An Era

Trains 13 and 14 "Nebraska Limited" departed Minneapolis and
Omaha the evening of September
29, 1965 and on the morning of
September 30 . . .

. . . the Chicago Great Western was
freight-only. An era of transportation which included names such
as RED BIRD, BLUE BIRD,
MILLS CITIES LIMITED, LE-
GIONNAIRE, GREAT WEST-
ERN LIMITED had come to an
end.

Five

CHICAGO GREAT WESTERN IN ILLINOIS

	Time Table No. 160 November 20, 1949 STATIONS DEPART		FIRST CLASS										
Distance from Chicago		Passing siding capacity in 45 foot cars	301	10	26	608	6	403	317	246	8	602	32
			Soo Line No. 1	B. & O. No. 10	B.& O. No. 26	C. & O. No. 8	B. & O. No. 6	C.G.W. No. 3	Soo Line No. 17	B. & O. No. 246	B. & O. No. 8	C. & O. No. 2	B. & O. No. 32
			DAILY	DAILY	DAILY	DAILY	DAILY	DAILY	DAILY	DAILY	DAILY	DAILY Except Saturday	DAILY
			A.M.	A.M.	P.M.	P.M.	P.M.	P.M.	P.M.	P.M.	P.M.	P.M.	P.M.
0.0	Chicago.......... 1.0		1.15	11.10	4.00	4.20 (6)	4.30 (608-403)	4.35 (6)	5.50	8.45	11.00	11.15	11.30
1.0	16th Street...... Chgo.Riv.Brg. 0.8		......	......	......	......	......	......	......	......	......	......	......
1.8	Halsted Street.... 0.5		1.23	11.13	4.03	4.23	4.33	4.38	5.53	8.48	11.03	11.18	11.33
2.3	Throop Street.... 0.9		1.25	11.14	4.04	4.24	4.34	4.39	5.54	8.50	11.04	11.19	11.34
3.2	Robey Yard....... 0.5		......	......	......	......	......	......	......	......	......	......	......
3.7	Western Ave. Jct.. C. & N.W. 0.5		1.28	11.16	4.06	4.26	4.36	4.41	5.56	8.52	11.06	11.21	11.36
4.2	Rockwell St....... C.N.W.-Pa.Co. 0.4		......	......	......	......	......	......	......	......	......	......	......
4.6	Sacramento Ave... 0.8		1.31	......	......	......	......	4.44	5.59	......	......	......	......
5.4	St. Louis Ave...... 0.4		......	......	......	......	......	......	......	......	......	......	......
5.8	Springfield Ave.... 0.8		......	......	......	......	......	......	......	......	......	......	......
6.6	Forty-Fifth Ave.... 0.3		......	......	......	......	......	......	......	......	......	......	......
6.9	Forty-Eighth Ave... 1.2		1.35	......	......	......	......	4.47	6.03	......	......	......	......
8.1	Central Ave....... 2.4		1.37	......	......	......	......	4.49	6.05	......	......	......	......
10.5	Chgo. Grt. West. Jct.... CA&E 0.5		1.40	......	......	......	......	4.55	6.10	......	......	......	......

CGW did not own its right-of-way in Chicago. Instead, it used the tracks of the Baltimore and Ohio Chicago Terminal Railroad (B&OCT). The track connection, named Chicago Great Western Junction, was located in Forest Park. CGW train crews were governed by B&OCT train orders, rules, and special instructions when operating on that railroad. This portion of B&OCT employee timetable No. 160, effective November 20, 1949, shows mileage and stations between Chicago Great Western Junction and Grand Central Station. (Author's collection.)

A CONTINUOUS JOURNEY

Between the East and all points North and West with no transfer at Chicago.

The **Grand Central Station** is the Western Terminus of the BALTIMORE & OHIO, LAKE SHORE & MICHIGAN SOUTHERN, and NICKEL PLATE Railroads, and the Eastern Terminus of the

CHICAGO GREAT WESTERN RAILWAY

CGW used a temporary depot at Fifth Avenue (Wells Street) and Polk Street in Chicago when it inaugurated passenger service in Illinois on July 31, 1887. It continued to use this facility until April 1, 1892, when it moved operations one block north to Grand Central Station. This advertisement was published in 1902. (Author's collection.)

This postcard view shows the famous Grand Central clock tower at the corner of Fifth Avenue (left) and Harrison Street (right). The tower height was 273 feet, and it contained a bell, inscribed, "I ring for all," that rang on the hour. Different railroad companies owned Grand Central over the years after the formal opening on December 8, 1890, but CGW was always a tenant. (Author's collection.)

Steam locomotive No. 913 was photographed in the Grand Central train shed at the head end of a passenger train. Solon Spencer Beman, architect, and Willis S. Jones, chief engineer of the Wisconsin Central Railroad, which owned the facility, designed what was called a "balloon shed," supported entirely by arches without intermediate supports. It was the second-largest balloon shed in the country after the New York Grand Central Station. (Joiner History Room, Sycamore, Illinois.)

This 1909 postcard scene shows the east side of Grand Central along Fifth Avenue. CGW passenger trains arrived and departed Grand Central continuously until the company ended passenger service in Illinois in August 1956. The station complex included the CGW Harrison Street freight house, located between Grand Central and the Chicago River. (Author's collection.)

A mechanic is performing repairs on a locomotive at Chicago Transfer Yard, the only CGW terminal freight yard in Chicago. It was located seven miles west of Grand Central, and its functions included making up freight trains, transferring freight cars, repairing freight cars, and servicing locomotives. CGW initially leased space at roundhouses on Twelfth Street (Roosevelt

Road) and Robey Street for servicing passenger and freight locomotives, respectively. Later the company built its own roundhouse for freight engines at Forty-sixth Street (Kenyon Avenue) just east of Chicago Transfer. Passenger power was then serviced at Robey Street. (Joseph Piersen.)

Steam locomotive No. 864 was photographed at the Forty-sixth Street roundhouse (background). Note the turntable behind the engine. Forty-sixth Street included a 100-ton capacity coal tipple and a 50,000-gallon water tank. (Author's collection.)

This photograph was taken from the cab of diesel engine No. 108-C as it arrived at Chicago Transfer Yard with a freight train on June 12, 1967. The yard was situated on leased property and was much smaller when M&NW began operations in Illinois in 1887. CGW expanded the size of the yard to increase capacity in 1900 and 1901 by purchasing land to the south. Chicago Transfer Yard was located north of Twelfth Street (Roosevelt Road) between Forty-eighth Street (Cicero Avenue) and Central Avenue, almost one mile in length. By 1907, it consisted of an eastbound yard between Forty-eighth Street and Fifty-second Street (Laramie Avenue) and a westbound yard between Fifty-second Street and Central Avenue. (Joseph Piersen.)

The Forty-sixth Street roundhouse was destroyed by fire on September 15, 1955, and CGW used a temporary facility until it built a new engine house in 1962 as part of a major reconstruction of Chicago Transfer Yard. This photograph shows the new locomotive servicing area at 12:30 a.m. on August 13, 1966. (Joseph Piersen.)

GP-30 locomotives are at the engine house on a winter day in the 1960s. The yard was also called Forty-eighth Street Yard, but Chicago Transfer Yard was an appropriate description. Arriving freight trains were broken apart at this facility, and cars were then classified either for interchange or delivery to local industries by the daily wayfreight. Most of the cars that were to be transferred to other railroads were interchanged with the Belt Railway, which provided intermediate switching service between carriers. The process worked in reverse for assembling outbound freight trains destined for the main yard at Oelwein. (Author's collection.)

GP-7 No. 120 was undergoing servicing at Chicago Transfer Yard when this photograph was taken in May 1967. CGW rebuilt and modernized the yard over a four-year period from 1959 to 1963. The company laid new track and constructed new freight car and locomotive repair facilities, a yard office, a pump house, a toolhouse, a sanding plant, fueling facilities, and a new "piggyback" ramp. (Author's collection.)

Forest Park was located three miles west of Chicago Transfer Yard. It was originally named Forest Home, and CGW constructed a depot here between 1912 and 1913. CGW trains crossed Des Plaines Avenue, streetcar tracks, and the Chicago, Aurora and Elgin Railroad (CA&E) at grade. A manned interlocking plant controlled train movements. Chicago Great Western Junction was located between Des Plaines Avenue and the CA&E crossing. The area was extensively changed between 1954 and 1960, when the Congress Street Expressway was constructed. This photograph shows CGW railcar M-1009 headed eastbound at the CA&E crossing in 1949, with the CGW depot in the background. Forest Park station was closed on May 19 of that year. (Author's collection.)

WESTBOUND				TIME TABLE No. 9 Effective January 20, 1957		Distance from Chicago	Station Numbers	Office Calls	HOURS OF TELEGRAPH SERVICE	
SECOND CLASS									Monday Thru Friday	Saturdays, Sundays, Holidays
91 Manifest Freight	**143** Manifest Freight									
Depart Daily	Depart Daily									
			PH	CHICAGO	7.3	0.0	425		6.00 AM to 2.00 PM 8.30 PM to 4.30 AM	6.00 AM to 2.00 PM 8.30 PM to 4.30 AM
11.00PM	12.01AM		PH-R	CHICAGO TRANSFER	3.0	7.3	417	JR		
11.45PM	12.15		PH	C.G.W. Jct. FOREST PARK	1.3	10.3	415	KC	Continuous	Continuous
			PH	MAYWOOD	1.5	11.6	414		7.00 AM to 3.00 PM 9.00 PM to 5.00 AM	7.00 AM to 3.00 PM 9.00 PM to 5.00 AM
12.45AM	12.25		PH-R	BELLWOOD	1.7	13.1	412	BQ	7.00 AM to 11.30 AM	
1.00	12.40		PH	ELMHURST	0.4	14.8	409	PR	12.30 PM to 4.00 PM	
				End of Two Main Tracks. I.C.R.R. Crossing		17.2				
1.20	1.00		PH	GRETNA		25.6	400	GA	7.00 AM to 12 Noon 1.00 PM to 4.00 PM	
1.30	1.30		PH-R	INGALTON	5.2	30.7	395	NI	6.15 AM to 11.30 AM 12.30 PM to 3.15 PM	6.15 AM to 11.30 AM 12.30 PM to 3.15 PM
1.40	1.40		PH	ST. CHARLES	3.0	35.9	390	SB	7.00 AM to 12 Noon 1.00 PM to 4.00 PM	
1.50	1.50		PH	WASCO	4.2	41.4	384	WO	8.00 AM to 12 Noon 1.00 PM to 5.00 PM	
2.00	2.00		PH	LILY LAKE	3.0	45.6	380			
2.05	2.06		PH	VIRGIL	8.0	48.6	377	VX	8.00 AM to 12 Noon 1.00 PM to 5.00 PM	(Saturday Only) 8.00 AM to 12 Noon 1.00 PM to 5.00 PM
2.20	2.20		PH-R	SYCAMORE	3.3	55.6	369	DX	8.00 AM to 12 Noon 1.00 PM to 5.00 PM	
			PH	C.M.St.P.&P. Crossing	2.2	61.9				
2.45	2.35		PH	CLARE	5.7	64.1	351	KU	8.00 AM to 12 Noon 8.45 PM to 12.30 AM	
2.55	2.45		PH	ESMOND	6.1	69.8	345	UY	1.30 AM to 5.45 AM 8.00 AM to 12 Noon	
3.05	2.55		PH	LINDENWOOD	3.5	74.9	340	WD	1.00 PM to 5.00 PM	
				C.B.&Q.Crossing						
3.15	3.02		PH	HOLCOMB	9.4	78.4	347		4.00 AM to 12 Noon	
3.35	3.20		PH-R	BYRON		87.8	337	BY	1.00 PM to 5.00 PM	
				C.M.St.P.&P.Crossing	6.0	88.3				
3.50	3.33		PH	MYRTLE		93.8	332			
4.05	3.45		PH	GERMAN VALLEY	5.8	100.9	325	GY	4.00 AM to 12 Noon 1.00 PM to 5.00 PM	
4.15	4.15		PH	SOUTH FREEPORT	13.3	106.7	319	DA	8.00 AM to 12 Noon 1.00 PM to 5.00 PM	
4.45	4.50		PH	PEARL CITY	9.0	120.0	306	BG	8.00 AM to 12 Noon 1.00 PM to 5.00 PM	
				End of Two Main Tracks.						
5.05	5.10		PH	EAST STOCKTON	2.7	120.0				
5.10	6.00		PH-R	STOCKTON	0.4	131.1	294	NS	6.00 AM to 2.00 PM 8.30 PM to 4.30 AM	6.00 AM to 2.00 PM 8.30 PM to 4.30 AM
5.15	6.30		PH	GOLDEN		131.5				
				End of Two Main Tracks.	11.8					
			PH	ELIZABETH		143.3	282	ZA	8.00 AM to 12 Noon 1.00 PM to 5.00 PM	
5.45	7.00		PH	NORTH HANOVER	3.3	146.6	279	AF	8.00 AM to 12 Noon 1.00 PM to 5.00 PM	
6.10	7.20		PH	AIKEN	8.8	155.4	269			
				End of Two Main Tracks.	2.2					
6.15	7.25		PH	GALENA JCT.		157.6	266	RQ	Continuous	Continuous
				End of Two Main Tracks.						
			PH	PORTAGE	0.5	158.1				
			PH	EAST CABIN	12.8	170.9		CB	Continuous	Continuous
				C.B.&Q. Crossings	0.4	171.3				
6.45	7.55		PH	DUBUQUE JCT.	0.6	171.9		JC	Continuous	Continuous
				C.M.St.P.&P. Crossing						
			PH	DUBUQUE		172.1	253			(Except Holidays) 5.00 AM to 1.00 PM 4.00 PM to 12 Mid.
7.01	8.10		PH-R	FAIR GROUND	1.1	174.2	251	RZ	5.00 AM to 1.00 PM 4.00 PM to 12 Mid.	
				End of Two Main Tracks.	13.7					
7.30	8.40		PH	GRAF	8.1	187.9	237			
7.55	9.00		PH	FARLEY	6.6	196.0	229		8.00 AM to 12 Noon	
8.05	9.15		PH	DYERSVILLE	8.1	202.5	223	DY	1.00 PM to 5.00 PM	
8.20	9.35		PH	ALMORAL	4.6	210.6	215			
				C.M.St.P.&P. Crossing	15.2	215.2	210			
8.50	10.25		PH	LAMONT	4.8	230.4	195	DJ	8.00 AM to 12 Noon 1.00 PM to 5.00 PM	
			PH	AURORA	7.3	235.2	190	OU	8.00 AM to 12 Noon 1.00 PM to 5.00 PM	
9.10	10.55		PH	FELTON		242.5				
				End of Two Main Tracks.	2.7					
				C.R.I.&P.Crossing	0.6	245.2				
9.20AM	11.01AM		PH-R-Ry	OELWEIN		245.5	160	WI	Continuous	Continuous
Arrive Daily	Arrive Daily					245.8				
10 20	11 00			Time on District						

Eastbound trains are superior to westbound trains of the same class. Rule 71.

This is the westbound schedule of CGW Eastern Division employee timetable No. 9, effective January 20, 1957. The reader may find it useful to locate stations and facilities as this book continue westward. (Author's collection.)

A westbound CGW freight train passes the Maywood depot, one mile west of Chicago Great Western Junction. M&NW opened a station here in 1887. The railroad received a substantial amount of business from American Can Company at Maywood, and it constructed the Seventeenth Avenue Yard to accommodate shipments. American Can signed a contract with CGW and Chicago Junction Railway (Indiana Harbor Belt Railroad or IHB) in 1897 to build a long spur track from the company's factory located one mile north of the CGW. Maywood station was closed on August 29, 1958. (Joseph Piersen.)

A SERIES OF CITY LEAGUE GAMES.

Whitings vs. Garden Citys.

A Grand Real Estate and Base Ball Excursion, Saturday, June 6th,

—TO—

BELLEWOOD.

A Special Through Excursion Train

WILL BE PROVIDED BY THE

Chicago, St. Paul & Kansas City R'y.

LEAVING GRAND CENTRAL DEPOT (Cor. Harrison-st. and Fifth-av.) at 2 P. M.

This Train will not stop at intermediate stations.

TICKETS (including railway fare) 25 CENTS APIECE.

Each Ticket has a Coupon attached, one of which is good for $1.00 to apply on any lot purchased on this Excursion at

| LOTS $125 WITH PLANK SIDEWALK, $5 Down, $5 Monthly. | BELLEWOOD | LOTS $175 WITH CLEVELAND STONE SIDEWALK, $7 Down, $7 Monthly. |

With the privilege of paying up as soon as purchaser wishes.

TIME CARD.

| 2:00 P. M. Leave Grand Central Depot. | 2:30 to 4:00 P. M. Real Estate Sale. | 6:00 P. M. Leave Bellewood. |
| 2:30 P. M. arrive at Bellewood. | 4:00 to 6:00 P. M. Base Ball Game. | 6:30 P. M. Arrive at Chicago. |

All Authorized Salesmen will wear Badges.

Free Excursion Sunday, June 7th. Office open until 9 P. M. daily.

BUTLER LOWRY (Ground Floor), 145 Washington-st.

Real estate developers established the first subdivisions in Bellwood during the 1890s, and baseball games were held to attract customers. CStP&KC provided excursion service, as shown in this *Chicago Tribune* newspaper advertisement from 1891. Note the early spelling of the subdivision name. The railroad constructed a depot at Bellwood in 1891, which was slightly more than a mile west of Maywood station. (Chicago Tribune.)

A predecessor company of the IHB signed an agreement in 1897 with CGW that allowed the Chicago, Hammond and Western Railroad (CH&W) to cross CGW at grade at Bellwood. The contract also included provisions on constructing an interchange track. This junction became one of the most important on the CGW because most of the eastbound perishable traffic was interchanged with the IHB at Bellwood. Also, CGW and IHB provided freight service at a stone quarry south of Bellwood. CGW steam locomotive No. 878, at the head end of a freight train, was photographed at Bellwood on November 12, 1937. (Author's collection.)

24. CLOSE CLEARANCES:

CHICAGO	Viaducts and trolley wires over various foreign line tracks in Chicago terminals used by C.G.W. trains, transfers and yard engines will not clear man on top or side of car.
BELLWOOD	IHB railway bridge will not clear man on top or side of car.
GALENA JCT.	Bridge over Galena River will not clear man on top or side of car.
MARSHALLTOWN	Guard against close clearances between main track and siding between First and Second Avenue. Between South track and adjacent tracks serving coal and oil companies.
TALMAGE	C.B.&Q. overhead bridge will not clear man on top or side of car.
CONCEPTION	Wabash overhead bridge will not clear man on top or side of car.

Special instructions were published in the 1957 employee timetable regarding close clearances at Bellwood. During 1930 and 1931, IHB elevated its tracks through the area, which then crossed over CGW. A wooden ramp was constructed from the elevated IHB main line to the interchange track at ground level. On March 11, 1949, the ramp, heavily coated with creosote, was destroyed by fire. It was rebuilt and returned to service on July 15, 1949. (Author's collection.)

A westbound CGW freight train powered by steam locomotive No. 879 is passing IHB interchange tracks at Bellwood in 1941. The volume of interchange business was substantial, and in 1965, CGW reported that it interchanged an average of 110 cars per day with the IHB at Bellwood. (Author's collection.)

The CGW main line in DuPage County near Elmhurst, four miles west of Bellwood, is shown on April 18, 1938, in a view facing east. CGW followed a policy of constructing a second main track for a distance of at least 10 miles out of important terminals to relieve congestion. It double-tracked the main line between Forest Park and Elmhurst in 1910. (M. D. McCarter Collection, negative No. N47658.)

Elmhurst station was first named South Elmhurst when M&NW started service here in 1887. The depot was constructed at that time and remained in service until the merger in 1968. Other facilities at Elmhurst included a water tank originally supplied from an artesian well 1,700 feet deep (the tank was later connected to the city water main). The depot and station grounds were purchased by the City of Elmhurst and developed into a public park called Wild Meadows Trace. This photograph was taken in 1961. (Joiner History Room, Sycamore, Illinois.)

Elmhurst, Ill.			
Alexander Lumber Co.	Coal-Building Material	C&NW	No
Bade, Edward, & Sons	Paper Products	C&NW	No
Building Supply Co.	Building Material	Team Track	
Davis Fuel Co.	Coal-Fuel	IC	Yes
Dramm Greenhouses, Inc.	Florist-Coal	IC	Yes
DuPage Feed & Supply Co.	Feed	Team Track	
Elmhurst-Chicago Stone Co.	Stone-Sand-Gravel	C&NW	No
Elmhurst College	Coal	Team Track	
Hammerschmidt & Franzen Co.	Lumber-Millwork	C&NW	No
Peoples Coal & Material Co.	Coal-Building Material	CGW	Yes
Standard Oil Co.	Petroleum Products	IC	Yes
Sturtevant, P. A., Co.	Manufacturing	Team Track	
Swanson Feed & Hardware	Feed-Poultry Supplies	Team Track	

CGW served few industries at Elmhurst. The company had an interchange here with the Illinois Central Railroad (IC), which crossed CGW at grade. (Author's collection.)

CGW constructed a siding one mile west of Elmhurst in 1910 to deliver construction materials for a new subdivision called Villa Park. In 1914, Villa Park was incorporated as the village of Ardmore. The name was changed to the village of Villa Park in 1917, partly because CGW tariffs referred to the community by this name. CGW constructed the Villa Park depot in 1926. It was closed on October 19, 1958, and sold to the community for use as a skaters' shelter at the village ice rink. The building is still owned by the village, and on May 14, 2001, Villa Park received a historic preservation plaque to recognize its efforts restoring the depot. (James L. Rueber.)

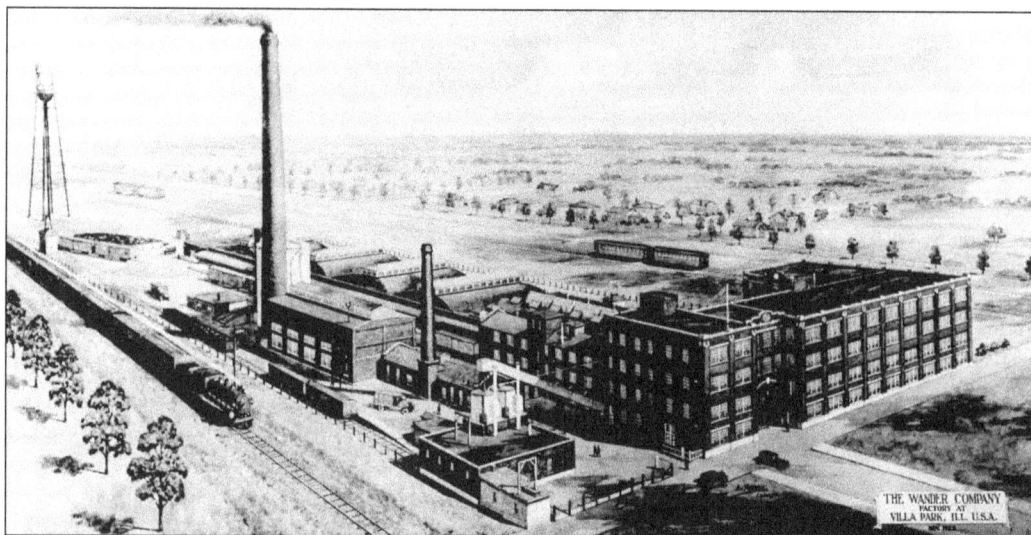

The Wander Company, manufacturers of Ovaltine, opened its only plant in the United States at Villa Park in 1917. CGW published an article on the facility in its company magazine, *The Maize*, and reported Wander was expected to ship and receive 200 carloads annually. Volume became substantial over the years, and CGW was handling between 500 and 600 carloads a year by 1961. This drawing of the plant was made in 1928, and it features a speeding westbound CGW freight train (left). (Villa Park Historical Society.)

Steam locomotive No. 725 was photographed switching freight cars at Villa Park in June 1934. (M. D. McCarter Collection, negative No. N31066.)

Villa Park, Ill.			
General Lumber Corp.	Lumber	Team Track	....
Hines, Edward, Lumber Co.	Lumber	CGW	No
Pioneer Garden Paint & Pet Supply	Salt	Team Track	....
Villa Park Coal & Material Co.	Coal	CGW	No
Wander Co., The	Beverage Preparation-Chemists	CGW-CA&E	No

This is a list of rail shippers at Villa Park. (Author's collection.)

On December 28, 1941, an eastbound CGW freight train derailed due to a broken axle while passing through Villa Park. Bacon, cuts of meat, soap, and grease were scattered about the depot as eight boxcars left the rails and broke open. Within minutes, motorists and bystanders were carrying away as much as they could! (James L. Rueber.)

CGW opened a station at Lombard, two miles west of the Villa Park depot, in 1887. It was closed on July 21, 1931, and company records show the railroad razed the structure in October 1957 because it "was old and beyond repair." (Lombard Historical Society.)

Lombard, Ill.			
Alexander Lumber Co.	Coal-Building Material	CGW	No
Du Page Community Builders, Inc.	Cement Blocks	Team Track	
Hammerschmidt Lumber & Fuel Co.	Coal-Building Material	C&NW	No
Lombard Floral Co., The	Flowers-Coal	CGW	No
Lombard Lumber Co.	Lumber-Building Material	Team Track	
Pure Oil Co.	Petroleum Products	CA&E	No
Westmore Supply Co.	Coal-Building Material	CA&E	No

Lombard industries were served by CGW. (Author's collection.)

SIDINGS AND SPURS BETWEEN STATIONS

	STATION NO.	MILE POST	CAR CAPACITY	CONNECTED
Villa Park	407	18.5	29	Both ends
Lombard	405	20.9	20	Both ends
North Glen Ellyn	402	23.3	3	West end
Campbell's Spur	394	29.7	15	East end
Fox River	388	37.3	97	Both ends
Five Points	365	59.3	15	East end
Stillman Valley	342	83.4	24	Both ends
Egan	329	96.7	27	Both ends
Bolton	311	114.3	25	East end
Kent	301	124.9	20	East end
Woodbine	287	138.6	21	Both ends
Rice	271	153.6	10	Both ends
Aiken Spur		155.1	9	East end
Durango	245	180.1	25	East end
Petersburg	217	207.5	32	Both Ends
Oneida	210	215.2	37	East end
Thorpe	220	220.2	5	East end
Dundee	200	225.3	15	West end
Stanley	185	239.7	28	Both Ends
DeKalb	7374	On branch 6 miles south of Sycamore Yard		

M&NW followed a policy of establishing local stations approximately every five miles while constructing its line through Illinois between 1886 and 1887. Some stations consisted of a depot and siding; others were only a platform or shed for shipping milk. Stations that were seldom patronized were eventually closed and the sidings left in place as passing tracks. The old station name remained in use, however, to identify the siding location. This list, published in the 1957 employee timetable, includes long-abandoned stations, such as North Glen Ellyn, which closed April 12, 1920. (Author's collection.)

Gretna, west of Lombard, was a small rural community when the M&NW started service here in 1887. Subdivisions were established in this area during the late 1950s, and the community was incorporated as the village of Carol Stream in 1959. CGW renamed the station accordingly in 1962. It remained in use by the railroad after the 1968 merger, and C&NW eventually sold the depot to the village. The structure was dismantled and reassembled at Armstrong Park, where it is now Gretna Station Museum. (Joiner History Room, Sycamore, Illinois.)

New plant of Container Corporation of America at Carol Stream, Illinois, served exclusively by the Chicago Great Western Railway Company.

Container Corporation of America opened the world's most modern folding-carton plant at Carol Stream in 1964. The facility was served exclusively by CGW. (Author's collection.)

M&NW constructed a depot, stockyard, and milk platform at Ingalton in the spring of 1887 on land donated by Theodore Schramer, a local farmer. The town of Ingalton developed around the depot, and it eventually consisted of a general store, blacksmith shop, and post office. It eventually became a ghost town after the post office closed in 1934. The first Ingalton depot was replaced with this Armco Steel structure in 1951. (Joiner History Room, Sycamore, Illinois.)

CGW had an interchange connection with the Elgin Joliet and Eastern Railroad (EJ&E) at Ingalton and a small freight yard with a wye track. Oversize shipments were interchanged here because EJ&E had ample clearance around the congested Chicago Switching District. The station continued in use after the 1968 merger, and the depot was not dismantled until the early 1980s. CGW steam locomotive No. 857 was photographed at Ingalton in September 1937. (James L. Rueber.)

An eastbound freight train is rushing past the depot at St. Charles, six miles west of Ingalton. M&NW began service at St. Charles in 1887, and the station developed into a complex of rail facilities, including a water tank, a milk shed, a supervisor's office, section hands' bunkhouses, toolsheds, and a signal maintainer's shed. CGW also owned the St. Charles Hotel and Park Company, incorporated in April 1889 to develop a summer resort hotel and picnic grounds along the west bank of the Fox River. The hotel was never built, some of the property was later platted for residences, and most of the land was sold in 1912 to St. Charles Township for continued use as a public park. The St. Charles Hotel and Park Company was dissolved on April 20, 1927. (Joiner History Room, Sycamore, Illinois.)

St. Charles, Ill.			
Chronicle Publishing Co., Inc.	Newsprint	Team Track	
Cities Service Oil Co.	Petroleum Products	CGW	No
Colonial Ice Cream, Inc.	Salt	Team Track	
Du Kane Corp.	Electrical Supplies	Team Track	
Fox Valley Box Co., Inc.	Paper Boxes	CGW	No
Gerdau Co.	Furniture	Team Track	
Hawley Products Co.	Paper Products	CGW	No
Hines, Edward, Lumber Co.	Building Supplies	CGW	No
Howell Co., Inc., The	Furniture	C&NW	No
Joshel, M. A., & Bros., Inc.	Lumber-Cement-Fuel	CGW	No
Kane Distributing Co.	Beverages	C&NW	No
Lindahl, S. C., Co.	Feeds	C&NW	No
McCormack Oil Co.	Petroleum Products	CGW	No
Moline Malleable Iron Co.	Castings	CGW	No
Owens Illinois Glass Co.	Plastic Products	C&NW	No
Parkers Builders Supplies	Fuel-Lumber	CGW	No
Roto Color, Inc.	Printers	CGW	No
St. Charles, City of	Coal-Salt	Team Track	
St. Charles Lumber & Fuel Co.	Fuel-Building Supplies	C&NW	No
St. Charles Manufacturing Co.	Cabinets	CGW	No

CGW served many shippers at St. Charles. Some of these businesses were located along a dangerous spur called the "hole track." It was constructed in 1891 and descended on a steep, curving grade from the elevated Fox River Bridge approach. CGW switchers "ran away" several times while descending the spur and ended up on Main Street at the end of track. The spur was removed during the early 1960s. (Author's collection.)

St. Charles, Ill.—Concluded			
Standard Oil Co.	Petroleum Products	CGW	No
State School for Boys	Supplies-Coal	C&NW	No
Stover Water Softener Co.	Water Softeners	CGW	No
United States Printing & Lithograph Co.....	Printers	CGW	No

Associates of the CGW promoted a manufacturing district on the west side of St. Charles in 1893. Several industries located here as well as a spur track that ran north three quarters of a mile to reach a stone quarry purchased by CGW in 1895. The railroad called this area West St. Charles and Fox River at various times, and records indicate a depot was also constructed here. (Author's collection.)

Architect's drawing of new institutional products plant to be built by General Mills, Inc., at St. Charles, Illinois, and to be served exclusively by Chicago Great Western.

General Mills purchased a 13-acre tract in the West St. Charles area from CGW in 1964 for a new institutional products plant. It was built in 1965 and featured a seven-story structure that housed storage bins. Rail shipments were handled exclusively by CGW. (Author's collection.)

A 1910 postcard view shows the first CGW Fox River Bridge at St. Charles constructed in 1886. A M&NW construction train was the first train to cross the bridge on December 31, 1886. (Author's collection.)

CGW replaced the bridge 70 years after it was built, when the railroad determined it was becoming structurally weak. Work began on August 10, 1956, and a new steel and concrete bridge 477 feet long was completed on January 4, 1957. This photograph shows an eastbound train about to cross the new bridge shortly after it was placed in service. St. Charles remained an open station after the 1968 merger, and the depot was not taken out of service until April 1983. Several organizations tried to raise funds to buy the building but were not successful, and C&NW tore down the structure in 1984. (Author's collection.)

A. B. Stickney, the company founder, reported in 1888 that most local stations were located on farms away from towns and villages. The company anticipated that the few residents in the area would provide sufficient business until a prosperous community developed, which would then depend upon the railroad for all of its transportation needs. This policy resulted in stations such as Wasco, opened in 1887 and closed on October 26, 1959. Wasco was located five miles west of St. Charles. (Joiner History Room, Sycamore, Illinois.)

Dispatchers' telephone also placed in waiting rooms of the following stations. These waiting rooms can be opened by switch key:

Lombard.	Esmond	North Hanover.
N. Glen Ellyn.	Lindenwood.	Aiken.
Gretna.	Stillman Valley.	Budd.
Wasco	Myrtle.	Petersburg.
Virgil.	Meekin.	Almoral.
Richardson.	Bolton.	Dundee.
Clare.	Woodbine.	Lamont.

Remote stations were not manned 24 hours a day, so train crews were provided with these instructions in case they had to contact their dispatcher from a closed depot. The instructions were published in Eastern Division employee timetable No. 22, effective June 4, 1922, for stations in Illinois and Iowa. (Chicago and North Western Historical Society.)

Form 19	**Chicago Great Western Railway**	Form 19
TRAIN ORDER NO. 6 3 6	FEBY 3 1×67	19

To
To. C&E WEST BOUND TRAINS ⁿ? CHGO TFR ILLS
To.
X _____ Operator. _____ M

   AT WASCO SIDING OUT OF SERVICE BETWEEN HOUSE TRACK
SWITCHES
AT SYCAMORE EXPECT TO FIND CARS ON EAST END OF SIDING
LOOK OUT FOR PILES OF DIRT AND TRACK MATERIAL
MP 77 - 10 TO MP 77 - 20

              NJK

_____DISPATCHER
CONDUCTOR AND ENGINEMAN MUST EACH HAVE A COPY OF THIS ORDER
MADE _____ TIME _____ M. _____ Opr.

CGW used a system of train dispatching called "timetable and train order." Train orders are instructions from the dispatcher communicated to the station operator, who then passes the information on to the engineer and conductor. The operator displays a signal when he has orders for an approaching train. There are two types of orders used. Form 19 is handed to the engineer and conductor, using a hoop, as the train passes. Form 31 requires the engineer to stop the train, and both he and the conductor must sign for the order. This Form 19 order was issued on February 3, 1967, to warn westbound train crews that Wasco siding was out of service and to watch out for obstructions farther west. (Conrad "Pete" Pedersen.)

Eastbound locomotive No. 874 with a freight train passes Lily Lake depot in 1943, slightly more than four miles west of Wasco. The first M&NW train order in Illinois was issued May 5, 1887, at Sycamore, instructing work trains to meet at Campton Pit, a stone quarry in Campton Township, east of Lily Lake. A station was opened at Lily Lake in 1887 and remained in service until it closed on December 7, 1951. (Joiner History Room, Sycamore, Illinois.)

(22). Telephones connected with Dispatchers' office are located at following passing track switches:

Gretna	West switch.
Ingalton	West switch.
St. Charles	East switch.
Fox River	Middle of Siding
Lily Lake	Extreme west switch.
Sycamore	Extreme east and west switches.
Wilkinson	East switch.
Holcomb	West switch.
Stillman Valley	West switch.
Byron	East and west switches.
South Freeport	East end south passing track.
	West end north passing track.
Bolton	West switch.
Pearl City	East switch.
Fair Ground	West switch.
Durango	East switch.
Graf	East and west switches.
Kidder	East switch.
Farley	West switch.
Dyersville	East switch.
Oneida	East switch.
Thorpe	West switch.
Lamont	East and west switches.

CGW also installed telephones at sidings for train crews to contact their dispatcher. This list of sidings in Illinois and Iowa, equipped with phones, was published in Eastern Division employee timetable No. 22, effective June 4, 1922. (Chicago and North Western Historical Society.)

This photograph shows a siding switch with a telephone box mounted on a pole in the background, west of Lily Lake. The numbers on the signal case are mileage from Chicago (top) and the number of the signal (bottom). (Joiner History Room, Sycamore, Illinois.)

This is a view of the right-of-way east of the Virgil depot, which is in the background to the left. CGW began to install its first automatic signals, semaphore type, between Forest Park and Aiken, Illinois, in April 1910 and completed the work in March 1911. The system was modernized starting in 1942, when CGW replaced the semaphore type with searchlight signals as shown. The upgrade was completed in 1947. (Joiner History Room, Sycamore, Illinois.)

CGW stations in rural Illinois typically consisted of a frame depot, livestock pen, and milk shed. The company also provided housing for the agent if none was available due to the remote location. These conditions applied at Virgil, three miles west of Lily Lake. The first station name was Virgil Center, and CGW reported that it had built a depot there in the company's 1897 annual report. Virgil was closed on February 28, 1962. (Joiner History Room, Sycamore, Illinois.)

At 5:00 p.m. on Saturday, August 22, 1953, a burned-out journal on a gondola loaded with coal caused a spectacular derailment east of Sycamore. The incident happened as westbound manifest No. 91 was traveling through at a fast rate of speed. Eighteen of 80 cars in the train went off the track and tore up 150 yards of track. While clearing away the wreckage, wrecker No. X200 was damaged and three crewmen injured when the 175-ton crane tipped over while lifting a heavily loaded boxcar. (Joiner History Room, Sycamore, Illinois.)

Most of the wreckage was removed by the following Wednesday, August 26. Several destroyed boxcars were set on fire to burn away all wood parts, and remaining metal parts were removed as scrap. (Joiner History Room, Sycamore, Illinois.)

Sycamore, eight miles west of Virgil, was an important and busy junction with facilities to service locomotives, freight yard, and online industries. It was also the site of a grade crossing and interchange with C&NW and a connection with the CGW branch to DeKalb. The railroad constructed a passenger depot here in 1887 (foreground) and a freight house in 1923 (right background). The 1968 merger did not have a major effect on business at Sycamore because C&NW operated its own line to this city from DeKalb. (Joiner History Room, Sycamore, Illinois.)

Locomotive No. 856 has stopped at Sycamore to replenish its water supply. Engine-servicing facilities included an engine house for the DeKalb switcher, a coal chute, and a water tank. Note the elevated flagman's shanty. (Joiner History Room, Sycamore, Illinois.)

CGW tore down the freight house and replaced it with this Armco Steel depot in 1951. The passenger depot was sold to a resident and moved off-site in March of that year. (Joiner History Room, Sycamore, Illinois.)

Eastbound locomotive No. 931, with a passenger train, has stopped at Sycamore to top off the tender water tank. O. T. Willard, the first CGW operator at Sycamore, often told the story of a fireman who fell into the tender. The only remark the engineer made when he found the fireman splashing around inside the tank was "John, we have enough water now. No need to get in and stamp it down!" (Joiner History Room, Sycamore, Illinois.)

The engineer of locomotive No. 856 is inspecting the engine's massive valve gear during a stop

at Sycamore. (Joiner History Room, Sycamore, Illinois.)

Sycamore, Ill.			
Anaconda Wire & Cable Co.	Wire	CGW	Yes
Arison Implement Co.	Implements	Team Track	
Arrow Feed Co.	Feeds	C&NW	No
B B Distributors	Beverages	C&NW	No
D-X Sunray Oil Co.	Petroleum Products	CGW	Yes
Dean Coal & Lumber Yard	Lumber-Fuel	CGW	Yes
DeKalb Agricultural Assn.	Feeds-Cattle	Team Track	
Diamond Wire & Cable Co.	Wire	CGW-C&NW	Yes
Driv Lok Pin Co.	Steel Specialties	C&NW	No
Duplex Products, Inc.	Printing	Team Track	
Farmers Grain & Lumber Co.	Feed-Building Supplies	CGW	Yes
Holcomb Yard	Fuel-Building Supplies	CGW	Yes
Holub Industries, Inc.	Electrical Supplies	Team Track	
Ideal Industries, Inc.	Electrical Supplies	Team Track	
Julep Co.	Syrups	Team Track	
Leader Oil Co.	Petroleum Products	C&NW	No

Anaconda Wire and Cable Company was Sycamore's largest industry, and it had five rail sidings. CGW published an article about the company in the November 1956 issue of *Safety News*. (Author's collection.)

Sycamore, Ill.—Concluded			
Micro Matic Hone Corp.	Specialties	CGW	Yes
Patten, J. V., Co.	Furnaces	CGW	Yes
Quinn Grain Co.	Grain	CGW	No
Socony Mobil Oil Co.	Petroleum Products	CGW	No
Standard Oil Co.	Petroleum Products	CGW	Yes
Stark, Frank	Livestock	C&NW	No
Sycamore, City of	Utilities	Team Track	
Sycamore Feed Yards, Inc.	Sheep	CGW	No
Sycamore Fuel Co.	Scrap Iron	C&NW	Yes
Sycamore Lumber Co.	Fuel-Building Supplies	C&NW	Yes
Sycamore Preserve Works, Inc.	Canners	C&NW	Yes
Sycamore Ready Mix	Concrete	C&NW	No
Turner Brass Works	Brass Goods	C&NW	Yes
Wells Lumber Co.	Building Supplies	Team Track	

Industries continued at Sycamore. Industrial development at this station, such as construction of a siding to wire works in 1893 and harvester works in 1900, was commented upon frequently in CGW annual reports. (Author's collection.)

The DeKalb and Chicago Great Western Railway (D&CGW), incorporated on March 23, 1895, constructed a six-mile branch from a connection with CGW at Sycamore south to DeKalb. CGW began operations over the branch in August 1895, and D&CGW was later sold to CGW on December 21, 1911. This old photograph, reproduced from a glass negative, shows the CGW depot at DeKalb. (Joiner History Room, Sycamore, Illinois.)

DeKalb, Ill.			
Builders Lumber & Supply	Building Supplies	C&NW	Yes
California Packing Corp.	Canners	C&NW	Yes
Chesney, John, Co.	Printers	Team Track	
City Fuel & Supply Co.	Fuel	CGW	Yes
Cortland DeKalb Yards	Elevator-Feed-Fuel	C&NW	Yes
Creamery Package Mfg. Co.	Milking Equipment	CMStP&P	Yes
Cyclone Fence Co., Division of United States Steel Corp.	Wire Cloth	CGW-C&NW	Yes
DeKalb Agricultural Assn., Inc.	Seeds	CGW-C&NW	Yes
DeKalb Commercial Body Corp.	Truck Bodies	C&NW	Yes
DeKalb County Grain Co.	Grain-Feed	C&NW	No
DeKalb Daily Chronicle	Newsprint	Team Track	
DeKalb Equipment Co.	Implements	Team Track	
DeKalb Ice Co.	Coal-Ice	C&NW	Yes
DeKalb Iron & Coal Co.	Scrap	CGW-C&NW	Yes
DeKalb Molasses Feed Co.	Feeds	C&NW	Yes
DeKalb Ogle Telephone Co.	Poles	Team Track	
DeKalb Phosphate Service	Rock-Phosphate	CGW	No
DeKalb Toy & Novelties Co.	Toys	Team Track	
Englander Co., Inc.	Bed Springs	CGW-C&NW	Yes
General Electric Co.	Electric Motors	CMStP&P	Yes
Hallgren Lumber & Coal Co., Inc.	Building Supplies	CGW-C&NW	Yes
Halverson Implement Co.	Implements	Team Track	
Heide Implement Co.	Implements	CGW	Yes
Hueber Quitno Farm Equipment	Implements	Team Track	
Hunt Feed Store & Mill	Feeds	CGW	Yes
Illinois State Highway Dept.	Salt	Team Track	
Johnson Concrete Co.	Concrete	C&NW	No
Kahle Oil Co.	Petroleum Products	CGW	No
Kishwaukee Service Co.	Petroleum Products	CGW-CMStP&P	No
McGirr Equipment Co.	Implements	Team Track	
Montgomery Ward & Co.	Merchandise	Team Track	
Nehring Electrical Works	Wire	C&NW	Yes
Newquist Foundry Co.	Castings	C&NW	Yes
Northern Illinois Produce Co.	Fruits-Vegetables	CGW	No
Northern Illinois State College	Coal	Team Track	
Northern Illinois Utilities	Power Plant	CGW	Yes

There were many shippers at DeKalb who routed freight by CGW, so it negotiated an agreement to use the C&NW line between Sycamore and DeKalb to continue service after it decided to abandon the DeKalb Branch. The ICC approved the plan on February 17, 1947. The last train operated over the DeKalb Branch in June of that year, and the rails were lifted in November. (Author's collection.)

A new junction developed near the R. N. Wilkinson farm, six miles west of Sycamore, when a predecessor company of the Chicago, Milwaukee, St. Paul & Pacific Railroad (CMStP&P) constructed a grade crossing there with CGW in 1905. The station was called Wilkinson, and it included a depot with an interlocking plant. It was closed on June 8, 1935, after an automatic interlocker was installed. (Joiner History Room, Sycamore, Illinois.)

M&NW established a station at Clare, two miles west of Wilkinson in 1887. A local newspaper reported in 1904 that the depot would be closed after CGW opened the nearby facility at Wilkinson. However, Clare remained open until August 29, 1958. (Joiner History Room, Sycamore, Illinois.)

Esmond, five miles west of Clare, was opened by M&NW in 1887, and it was still manned by an agent in 1969. The depot was closed sometime before C&NW abandoned this section of the old CGW in 1981. CGW built a residence for the Esmond agent in 1910 that consisted of two old bunk cars covered with a new roof. The dwelling was dismantled in 1953. (Joiner History Room, Sycamore, Illinois.)

Lindenwood, six miles west of Esmond, was placed in service by M&NW in 1887. Livestock shipments may have been the primary business here during the early years because CGW built an addition to the station sheep shed in 1893. The depot was damaged by fire in 1908, repaired, and remained in service until closed August 27, 1958. (Joiner History Room, Sycamore, Illinois.)

The Chicago, Burlington and Quincy Railroad (CB&Q) crossed CGW at grade at Holcomb station, three miles west of Lindenwood, and there was an interchange connection between the two railroads. Holcomb station was opened in 1887 and closed on March 20, 1950. (Joiner History Room, Sycamore, Illinois.)

Holcomb, Ill.			
Neidlinger Elevator	Grain-Fuel-Building Supplies	CGW-CB&Q	Yes
Ogle Service Co.	Feeds	Team Track	....

A grain elevator was erected near the CGW main line in 1897, and it provided most of the business at Holcomb. A second industry, Custom Farm Service, also located a facility here in 1967. All shipping transactions were handled at Byron since Holcomb depot was closed by this time. (Author's collection.)

CGW must have handled a significant amount of livestock business at Stillman Valley, five miles west of Holcomb, because the company modernized its stockyard there in 1928 by adding a second pen with sheds and a stock scale. The station was opened by M&NW in 1887, and it included a depot and toolhouse. (Joiner History Room, Sycamore, Illinois.)

Stillman Valley, Ill.			
Clark, J. L., Mfg. Co.	Metal Products	Team Track	
Rosensteil & Co.	Fuel-Grain-Feed	CGW	No
Stillman Valley Elevator	Grain	CMStP&P	No

The primary shipper at Stillman Valley was a grain elevator and feed dealer. The depot was closed July 22, 1931, and in 1943, it was dismantled and replaced by what CGW called a "frame shelter," as shown in the photograph. (Joiner History Room, Sycamore, Illinois.)

M&NW constructed this bridge across the Rock River in 1886. It consisted of five 143-foot deck truss spans and two 35-foot deck plate girder spans. This old photograph shows the bridge under repair during the early 1900s. (Author's collection.)

The first Rock River Bridge was replaced with this 12-span deck plate girder type in 1958. (Joiner History Room, Sycamore, Illinois.)

Byron, approximately four miles west of Stillman Valley, was a busy junction with a grade crossing and interchange connection with CMStP&P, sidings to several industries and a gravel pit, and locomotive servicing facilities. M&NW opened a station here in 1887, and Byron became a division point until CGW opened its East Stockton terminal in 1911. The station at Byron remained open after the 1968 merger and was not closed until May 1978. (Byron Museum of History.)

Byron, Ill.			
Auker Bros.	Livestock	Team Track	
Bainbridge Cattle Co.	Livestock	CGW	No
Barker Lumber Co.	Lumber-Fuel	CMStP&P	Yes
Blackhawk Builders Supply Co.	Building Supplies	Team Track	
Byron Cheese Co.	Cheese	Team Track	
Byron Elevator & Supply Co.	Feeds-Building Supplies	CGW	Yes
Byron Sand & Stone Co.	Gravel-Sand	CMStP&P	Yes
General Telephone Co. of Illinois	Poles	Team Track	
Illinois State Highway Dept.	Salt	Team Track	
Ogle County Marketing Assn.	Livestock	CMStP&P	No
Standard Oil Co.	Petroleum Products	CGW	Yes
Stevens Mfg. Co.	Metal Products	Team Track	
Walker Implement Co.	Implements	Team Track	

Milk and dairy products were an important source of business at Byron during the early years. CGW operated a milk train between Byron and Chicago that transported an average of 850 cans of milk a day by 1890. Also, an icehouse was constructed in 1891 to provide ice to keep the milk cold while in transit. The CGW 1914 annual report noted that a milk bottling plant with a capacity of 40,000 pounds of milk per day was in operation at Byron at this time. (Author's collection.)

The main line across Illinois mostly traversed farmland, and CGW constructed stone rail-top cattle crossings at many locations. The standard crossing measured six feet by six feet. (Author's collection.)

M&NW established a station at German Valley, 14 miles west of Byron, in 1887. At that time, there was a general store and one or two houses in the area. A village was platted in August 1887, and by 1910, the town had grown to include half a dozen stores, a creamery, a blacksmith shop, and the H. A. Hillmer Company grain elevator. German Valley was also the site of a terrible accident. A speeding westbound passenger train derailed in 1907, resulting in three fatalities. The accident was so severe that a mail car broke in two, and one section went through the lower floor of the grain elevator. German Valley was still open in 1969 but closed before the former CGW line was abandoned here in 1972. (Joiner History Room, Sycamore, Illinois.)

M&NW operated its trains over the IC between Dunbar, Illinois, and Dubuque from 1887 to 1888, when its own line in Illinois was completed. The station name was changed to South Freeport by 1891. The station, five miles west of German Valley, was an important interchange because IC delivered as many as 50 carloads of coal per day here from mines in southern Illinois for CGW steam locomotives. CGW owned coal mines and leased mining rights in Perry, Randolph, and Washington Counties through a subsidiary, Great Western Coal Company, which was incorporated on April 27, 1918. South Freeport depot closed on August 23, 1958, but the interchange remained open until it was abandoned in 1972. Great Western Coal Company was dissolved in 1960. (Joiner History Room, Sycamore, Illinois.)

M&NW established a station 14 miles west of South Freeport in 1887 and named it Yellow Creek because it was a quarter of a mile south of a small village with that name. A new community developed around the station, and merchants relocated their businesses from Yellow Creek closer to the station. A number of progressive citizens, feeling that it was inappropriate to use the same name for their new town, changed it to Pearl City in 1895. CGW also changed the station name as well. The depot was partially destroyed by a derailment, and it was replaced with this small concrete structure in 1953. Pearl City was closed on September 1, 1962. (Joiner History Room, Sycamore, Illinois.)

M&NW built a depot at Kent, five miles west of Pearl City, in December 1887, and a town with the same name was soon surveyed and platted near the station. Railroad facilities at Kent included a water tank, which was dismantled and removed by 1916. CGW double-tracked the main line from Kent to Galena Junction in 1910 and later removed the second set of tracks during the early 1950s. The depot at Kent was closed on July 9, 1951, and replaced with this shelter. (Joiner History Room, Sycamore, Illinois.)

In 1910, CGW constructed a new division point and crew change point four miles west of Kent and a mile east of Stockton, which replaced Byron. The facility was named East Stockton, and it was placed in service on January 15, 1911. The terminal consisted of a rail yard, roundhouse, water tank, coal chute, car shop, and dispatcher's office that controlled train movements between Oelwein and Chicago. There were 65 steam locomotives assigned to East Stockton, which operated between the division point and Chicago and Oelwein. One hundred and fifty people were eventually employed there, and the annual payroll reached $300,000 in 1929. This scene is a 1920 postcard view of East Stockton. (Author's collection.)

Coal Chute, East Stockton, Ill. 11806-R

The fleet of Texas-type 2-10-4 steam locomotives acquired in 1930 were capable of operating between Chicago and Oelwein with only intermediate stops for fuel and water. The roundhouse and shops at East Stockton were no longer needed, and the terminal was phased out between 1930 and 1936. The vacated property was later sold to the City of Stockton. This is a postcard scene of East Stockton in 1911. (Author's collection.)

M&NW acquired property from several farmers in Stockton Township, Jo Daviess County, for a depot and station in 1887. One of the farmers was Marvin Freeman Carpenter, who platted a village near the station, which incorporated on April 17, 1890, as the village of Stockton. CGW began to expand its facilities at the station, which eventually included water tanks, coal chutes, and a rail yard. This postcard view faces east from the Main Street viaduct. The depot is to the left, the water plant is in the left background, and the coal chute is in the center background. These facilities were dismantled after East Stockton opened. (James L. Rueber.)

This is a 1910 postcard view of the depot at Stockton with the crew of a westbound freight train posing casually for the camera. (Author's collection.)

View in Railroad Yards, Stockton, Ill.

This 1909 postcard scene is from the Stockton rail yard facing west. The Main Street viaduct and depot are in the background. CGW replaced the water tanks at Stockton in 1935 and 1936. (James L. Rueber.)

This photograph shows a westbound CB&Q passenger train on the CGW main line passing through Stockton. CGW allowed CB&Q to use its tracks as a detour when flooding along the Mississippi River placed the CB&Q main line out of service in April 1965. The two-story structure to the left is the old East Stockton dispatcher's office, which was relocated to Stockton in August 1931. It remained in use years later as a yard office after CGW consolidated all dispatching activity at Oelwein in 1949. The building was torn down and replaced with an office trailer in August 1971. C&NW closed Stockton station in March 1973. (Joiner History Room, Sycamore, Illinois.)

CGW locomotive engineer Frank Mininni salvaged the bell from steam locomotive No. 721, which was scrapped in 1950. In 1967, he donated the bell to the Stockton Park Board, which placed it on display at the community swimming pool. CGW reported on the donation in an article published in *Safety News*. The company informed readers that the bell was heard hundreds of times as No. 721 hauled many countless tons of freight in and out of Stockton. (Author's collection.)

M&NW constructed a depot at Woodbine, seven miles west of Stockton, in 1887. The station included a depot, toolhouse, stockyard, and water tank. The tank was removed prior to 1916, and Woodbine closed on April 23, 1951. (Joiner History Room, Sycamore, Illinois.)

Elizabeth station was located five miles west of Woodbine. M&NW constructed the depot here in 1887, and the facility included a water tank, which was abandoned and dismantled by 1916. Elizabeth closed in November 1969. The depot has since been restored and is now the Elizabeth Depot Museum. (Author's collection.)

M&NW opened a station named Trousdale three miles west of Elizabeth in 1887. The name was changed to North Hanover during the 1890s. It was also the junction with the Hanover and Great Western Railway, incorporated in February 1898 for the purpose of building and operating a two-and-a-half-mile branch between the CGW at North Hanover and the Hanover Woolen Mills in the village of Hanover. CGW constructed an elaborate water station at North Hanover in 1912 that drew water from the Apple River and replaced water stations at Woodbine, Elizabeth, and Rodden. The depot was replaced in 1914. The Hanover railroad ceased operations in 1934. (Joiner History Room, Sycamore, Illinois.)

This is a 1940 view of the east portal of Winston Tunnel, about six miles west of Elizabeth. CStP&KC started construction of the tunnel at the west heading on May 12, 1887, and from the east in July 1887. The headings met on December 22 of that year. The first train to pass through the tunnel was a construction train on January 19, 1888. CGW had to install a forced draft system in 1913 to improve ventilation due to the operation of the 2-6-6-2 Mallet-type locomotives, which operated at slow speed and exhausted a tremendous amount of gas and soot. Winston Tunnel was 2,440 feet in length, and passage through this long, narrow bore in a creeping Mallet was unbearable and dangerous for the train crew. (James L. Rueber.)

No. 671,264. Patented Apr. 2, 1901.
C. S. CHURCHILL & C. C. WENTWORTH.
MEANS FOR VENTILATING TUNNELS.
(No Model.) (Application filed Nov. 10, 1900.) 3 Sheets—Sheet 1.

Fig. 1.

Witnesses:-
M.M. Miles;

Inventors:
Charles S. Churchill.
Charles C. Wentworth.
by their Attorneys:-

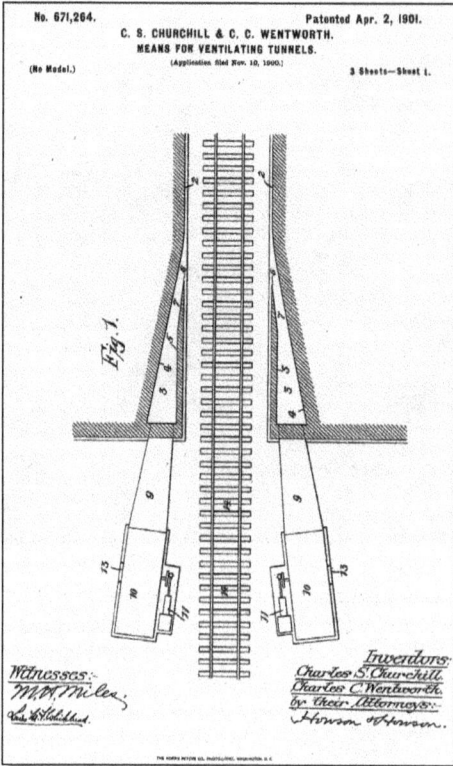

The company based the forced-draft system on the patented "Churchill method of ventilation." Patent sheet No. 1 of this device is shown. Two blowers or fans were situated on each side of the track with a ductwork system that directed forced air into a large chamber attached to the tunnel. An operator would start the blowers as a steam locomotive entered the chamber. Smoke and fumes would be directed ahead of the engine away from the cab. (Author's collection.)

No. 671,264. Patented Apr. 2, 1901.
C. S. CHURCHILL & C. C. WENTWORTH.
MEANS FOR VENTILATING TUNNELS.
(No Model.) (Application filed Nov. 10, 1900.) 3 Sheets—Sheet 2.

Fig. 2.

Witnesses:-
M.M. Miles;

Inventors:
Charles S. Churchill.
Charles C. Wentworth.
by their Attorneys:-

Sheet No. 2 shows the blower (left) with ductwork affixed to the tunnel (right). CGW used only one blower, a Sturtevant multivane fan, which delivered 280,000 cubic feet of fresh air per minute into the tunnel. (Author's collection.)

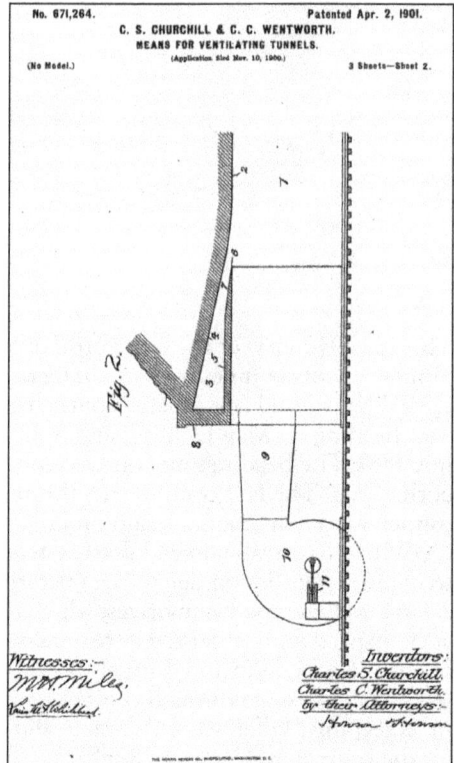

Sheet No. 3 shows how the chamber enclosed the portal. (Author's collection.)

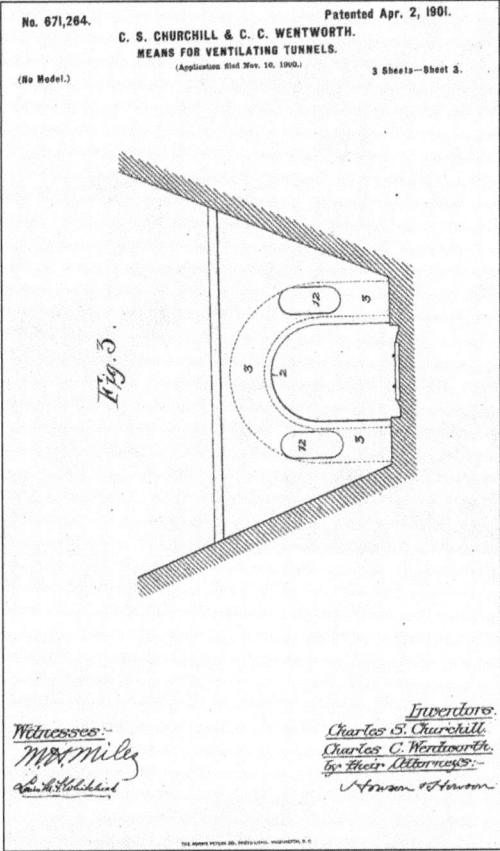

No. 671,264.   Patented Apr. 2, 1901.
C. S. CHURCHILL & C. C. WENTWORTH.
MEANS FOR VENTILATING TUNNELS.
(Application filed Nov. 10, 1900.)
(No Model.)   3 Sheets—Sheet 3.

Fig. 3.

Witnesses:—

Inventors.
Charles S. Churchill.
Charles C. Wentworth.
by their Attorneys:—

CGW powered the fan with a 180-horsepower diesel engine housed inside a two-story brick building (called a fanhouse), as shown in this old photograph. Note the blower and the duct and chamber, which the company called a "nozzle." It was a large steel and wood structure similar to an arched train shed roof, supported on concrete footings and positioned against the tunnel portal. The rectangular-shaped structure on the roof of the fanhouse was a cooling tower supplied from a well on the opposite side of the tracks. (James L. Rueber.)

This photograph shows the nozzle and cooling tower before the fanhouse was constructed. Note the site of the fanhouse has been cleared and graded prior to construction. There was an ascending, eastbound grade inside the tunnel, which forced locomotives to work harder and produce more smoke and fumes while inside. Ventilation was not required for westbound trains, which could drift downgrade with throttle closed. Therefore, a ventilation plant was installed only at the west end of Winston Tunnel. (James L. Rueber.)

This illustration depicts the diesel engine used to power the blower. CGW did not identify the manufacturer in its records, but the engine was similar to the Fairbanks Morse Type Y power plant developed in 1912 for industrial and agricultural applications. (James L. Rueber.)

The tunnel builders found a layer of limestone above the site and supposed the tunnel would be bored through solid rock. They were mistaken and, as the tunnel was excavated, they realized that it would have to be built through hard blue shale. This material rapidly disintegrates on exposure to air and water, which made Winston Tunnel unstable and prone to cave in. CGW relined the bore with brick and concrete and made other improvements over a two-year period from 1902 to 1904. This photograph shows a mason gang repairing the tunnel ceiling. The workers stood on top of boxcars, and wet cement was passed up to them through the opened hatch. (Author's collection.)

This is another view of the 1902 tunnel-relining project. (Author's collection.)

Steam locomotive No. 146 was used to position boxcars and other work cars inside the tunnel during repairs. (Joiner History Room, Sycamore, Illinois.)

The tunnel cost $600,000 to build, and CGW continued to spend large sums of money in repair and maintenance over the years. This view shows the west portal with additional structures added to the fanhouse. CGW closed this facility in the early 1950s after CGW converted its motive power fleet to diesel-electric. Ventilation was not needed because the diesel locomotive cab is in front and ahead of the exhaust stacks. C&NW operated the last train through Winston Tunnel on October 31, 1971, and it was abandoned the following year. The site is now owned by the Illinois Department of Natural Resources (IDNR) and administered as a unit of Apple River Canyon State Park. (Donald Vaughn.)

BETWEEN STOCKTON AND GALENA JUNCTION.—45 miles per hour for passenger trains and 25 miles per hour for freight trains on descending grades and curves.

WINSTON TUNNEL.—Westbound trains twenty miles per hour. Eastbound trains, when fan is running, ten miles per hour. Fan out of service, twenty miles per hour.

GALENA JUNCTION.—25 miles per hour for passenger trains and 15 miles per hour for freight trains over Junction switches.

Trains crews operating through Winston Tunnel had to comply with speed limits as shown in Eastern Division employee timetable No. 22, effective June 4, 1922. Note that the railroad allowed a higher speed when the fan was out of service to permit crews to exit as quickly as possible. (Chicago and North Western Historical Society.)

This photograph shows Rice station, February 3, 1931. CGW installed an electric staff system to control train movements through Winston Tunnel during the relining project in 1902. This train control system was retained after the project was completed, and it was later extended in 1905 between two new stations, Winston and Rice, east and west of the tunnel portals, respectively. The staff system remained in service for 26 years. CGW was one of the very few railroads in the United States that used this method of train control. It was replaced in 1931 with a centralized traffic control installation operated from a new addition to the fanhouse. The upgrade allowed CGW to close the staff stations at Winston and Rice on February 11, 1931. (James L. Rueber.)

DUBUQUE DISTRICT—Westward

Mile Posts	STATIONS	FIRST CLASS 11 The Hawkeye	FIRST CLASS 13 The Land O' Corn		SECOND CLASS 79 Dispatch CFS-3	SECOND CLASS 75 Dispatch CAC-5	SECOND CLASS 61 Freight	SECOND CLASS 71 Dispatch CC1	SECOND CLASS 77 Dispatch CW1	SECOND CLASS 73 Dispatch
	TIME TABLE NO. 24 Taking Effect October 25, 1959									
114.4	....FREEPORT..... 2.4	L 12 50AM	L 7 13PM	----------	----------	----------	----------	----------	----------	----------
		Daily	Daily		Daily	Daily	Daily	Daily	Daily	Daily
116.8	C WEST JUNCTION 5.5	L 12 55AM	L 7 18PM	----------	L 12 05AM	L 1 45AM	L 4 25AM	L 7 40AM	L 9 00AM	L 3 00PM
122.3	......ELEROY....... 4.6	1 01	7 24	----------	12 14	1 52	4 35	7 47	9 07	3 07
126.9	C......LENA........ 4.1	f 1 06 78	n 7 28	----------	12 21	1 58	4 41	7 53	9 13	3 13
131.0	..WADDAMS GROVE.. 4.0	1 10	7 32	----------	12 26	2 03	4 46	7 58	9 18	3 18
135.0	.......NORA....... 3.5	1 14	7 36	----------	12 31	2 07	4 51	8 03	9 23	3 23
138.5	D.... WARREN...... 6.0	s 1 20	s 7 41	----------	12 46 78	2 11	5 08	8 07	9 30 14	3 27
144.5	D..APPLE RIVER... 8.2	f 1 26	n 7 48 72	----------	12 53	2 17	5 20	8 14	9 38	3 35
152.7	C.SCALES MOUND. 5.5	1 34	n 7 56	----------	1 02	2 27	6 06 76	8 23	9 47	4 03 74
158.2	...COUNCIL HILL.. 6.4	1 43	8 04	----------	1 19	2 37	6 24	8 35	9 57	4 15
164.6	......GRANT....... .9	1 53	8 13	----------	1 38	3 07 12	6 46	8 59 14	10 09	4 29
165.5	D....GALENA....... 3.3	s 2 02	s 8 16	----------	1 41	3 23	6 52	9 03	10 13	4 32
168.8	C....PORTAGE..... 12.7	2 08	8 22	----------	1 48	3 30	7 15	9 10	10 20	4 39
181.5	C...EAST CABIN.... .2	2 22	8 35	----------	2 05	3 46	7 40	9 26	10 40	4 52
181.7	..EAST DUBUQUE.. .6	2 25	f 8 37	----------	2 07	3 48	7 45	9 28	10 43	4 54
182.3	C.DUBUQUE JCT... .9	2 29	8 41	----------	2 13	3 52	7 50	9 32	11 01 60	4 58
183.2	.....DUBUQUE.....	s { 2 35 / 2 50 } 12	s 8 45	----------	2 15	3 58	8 33 14	9 38	11 06	5 03

CGW connected with CB&Q at Aiken and operated over that railroad along the Mississippi River north one mile to Portage and a connection with the IC. CGW trains ran on IC almost 13 miles to Dubuque and a connection with the company's own rails. The CB&Q connection was changed to Galena Junction in 1902. CGW train crews were governed by CB&Q and IC train orders, rules, and special instructions when operating on these lines. This image shows stations and sidings between Portage and Dubuque published in IC employee timetable No. 24, effective October 25, 1959. (Author's collection.)

This CGW illustration from the 1890s shows the IC main line between Portage and Dubuque. (Author's collection.)

On Main Line of the Chicago Great Western Railway, approaching the city of Dubuque, on the bank of the Mississippi River.

Railroad Tunnel at East Dubuque, Ill.   81797

IC passed through a small tunnel at East Dubuque just before crossing the Mississippi River. This old postcard scene shows a westbound train exiting the tunnel headed toward Dubuque. (Author's collection.)

RAILROAD AND WAGON BRIDGES, LOOKING TOWARD DUBUQUE.

CGW crossed the Mississippi River over the IC bridge. This 1916 postcard view shows the railroad bridge (left) and Dubuque (background). (Author's collection.)

At the end of every CGW freight train was a caboose, which is an appropriate image for ending this chapter. This illustration of caboose No. 636 was published in the company's 1963 annual report. (Author's collection.)

Six

MERGER

Chicago
GREAT WESTERN Railway

SAFETY NEWS

JUNE 30, 1968

| VOLUME 14 FINAL ISSUE | Issued by the Chicago Great Western Railway Co. Oelwein, Iowa | V. Allan Vaughn, Editor G. L. Vargason, Ass't Editor |

Kansas City, Missouri

TO ALL GREAT WESTERNERS:

When the clock passes midnight on June 30th, a new era in transportation will begin as the Chicago Great Western Railway Company, through merger, combines its properties and operations with those of the Chicago and North Western Railway Company. The combined companies will span a 12,000 mile network from Chicago to the Dakotas, and from St. Louis and Kansas City to the Canadian Gateway at Duluth-Superior.

The Great Western enters this merger not only with its rolling stock and properties, but with its people, the heart of any company. When I think of the Great Western family, I cannot find words to describe the teamwork which has always characterized our Company. No task too difficult, no problem left unsolved, the team spirit has always been "give us results."

Good will between a corporation and the members of its family is a valued and respected factor, and the Great Western brings to the merged company the immeasurable experience, skills, spirit of cooperation and determination of each of you.

I know that the sincere trust and ability you have shown me will receive equal appreciation from the officers and staff of the merged company.

★

E. T. Reidy

On June 30, 1968, just before CGW ceased to exist, the company sent employees the last issue of *Safety News* with a farewell message from company president Edward T. Reidy. (Author's collection.)

CHICAGO & NORTH WESTERN RAILWAY

DES MOINES AND CENTRAL IOWA RAILWAY

MISSOURI DIVISION

TIMETABLE

No. 1

Effective January 1, 1969

AT 12:01 A. M.
CENTRAL STANDARD TIME

The entire CGW system became the C&NW Missouri Division on merger day, July 1, 1968. C&NW began to integrate train operations, close redundant facilities, and phase in CGW motive power into the C&NW fleet during the remainder of the year. The process was approaching completion when C&NW issued the first Missouri Division employee timetable No. 1, effective January 1, 1969. It contained schedules for all of the former CGW lines with special instructions that combined C&NW and CGW operating practices. (Author's collection.)

Westward—Stockton Subdivision—Eastward

SECOND CLASS			191	Mile Posts	Distance from Chicago		Timetable No. 1 January 1, 1969		Distance from Galena Jct.	Capacity of Sidings	192	SECOND CLASS		
			Tuesday Thursday Saturday				STATIONS				Monday Wednesday Friday			
					0		................CHICAGO................		157.6					
			—A.M.— 11.00		7.3	DQ	......CHICAGO TRANSFER.........	Y	150.3		—A.M.— A 2.40			
			—A.M.— 11.20	10.3	10.3	C	........FOREST PARK..........		147.3		—A.M.— A 2.20			
			11.30	13.1	13.1		...........BELLWOOD...........		144.5		2.10			
			11.37	16.8	16.8		..........ELMHURST...........		140.8	43	1.50			
			11.40	18.5	18.5		..........VILLA PARK..........		139.1		1.45			
			11.45	20.9	20.9		...........LOMBARD...........	Y	136.7		1.40			
			11.55	25.6	25.6	D	......CAROL STREAM........		132.0		1.30			
			12.05	30.7	30.7	DQ	..........INGALTON..........		126.9	87	1.20			
			12.15	35.9	35.9	D	........ST. CHARLES........		121.7	96	1.10			
			12.20	37.3	37.3		..........FOX RIVER..........		120.3	97	1.07			
			12.28	41.4	41.4		...............WASCO...........		116.2	65	12.59			
			12.36	45.6	45.6		..........LILY LAKE..........		112.0	52	12.51			
			12.42	48.6	48.6		.............VIRGIL..........		109.0		12.45			
			1.20	56.6	56.6	DQ	..........SYCAMORE..........	Y	101.0	222	12.30			
			1.25	59.3	59.3		.........FIVE POINTS.........		98.3		11.47			
			1.35	64.1	64.1		...............CLARE...........	Y	93.5		11.37			
			1.45	69.8	69.8	D	...........ESMOND...........	Y	87.8	138	11.27			
			1.55	74.9	74.9		..........LINDENWOOD..........	Y	82.7		11.17			
			2.05	78.4	78.4		...........HOLCOMB...........		79.2	55	11.10			
			2.15	83.4	83.4		.......STILLMAN VALLEY........		74.2		11.01			
			2.25	87.8	87.8	DQ	............BYRON............	Y	69.8		10.53			
			2.40	96.7	96.7		...............EGAN...........		60.9		10.37			
			2.50	100.9	100.9	D	......GERMAN VALLEY..........		56.8		10.30			
			3.10	106.7	106.7		........SOUTH FREEPORT.........	Y	50.9	222	10.20			
			3.25	114.3	114.3		.............BOLTON..........		43.3		9.42			
			3.35	120.0	120.0		.........PEARL CITY.........		37.6		9.32			
			3.50	124.9	124.9		...............KENT...........		32.7		9.24			
			4.05	129.0	129.0		.......EAST STOCKTON.........		28.6		9.16			
			4.15	131.1	131.1	DQ	..........STOCKTON..........	Y	26.5		9.10			
			4.20	131.5	131.5		.............GOLDEN..........		26.1		9.00			
			4.35	138.6	138.6		...........WOODBINE...........		19.0		8.46			
			4.48	143.3	143.3	D	.........ELIZABETH..........		14.3		8.39			
			4.55	146.6	146.6		.......NORTH HANOVER........		11.0	222	8.33			
			5.10	153.6	153.6		...............RICE...........		4.0		8.19			
			A 5.20 P.M.	157.6	157.6		..........GALENA JCT..........	Y	0		8.10 P.M.			

Between Chicago (Grand Central Station) and Forest Park trains operate over
  track of B&OCT RR. B&OCT timetable and rules govern.

The former CGW main line in Illinois was designated the Stockton Subdivision of the Missouri Division, and it was changed to the Stockton Subdivision of the C&NW Galena Division by May 1969. C&NW terminated the trackage agreement with B&OCT and closed Chicago Transfer Yard in October 1969. The old CGW main line became a long spur track served by wayfreights dispatched from C&NW terminals over existing interchanges or new connections. Most of the former CGW main line in Illinois was abandoned during the next 30 years. As of early 2006, only two short sections of former CGW right-of-way remain in operation in Illinois between West Chicago and St. Charles and at Byron. (Author's collection.)

Visit us at
arcadiapublishing.com

www.ingramcontent.com/pod-product-compliance
Lightning Source LLC
Chambersburg PA
CBHW080610110426
42813CB00006B/1463